The Critical Reception
of Howard Nemerov

A Selection of Essays
and a Bibliography

Edited by
BOWIE DUNCAN
with an introduction by
Reed Whittemore

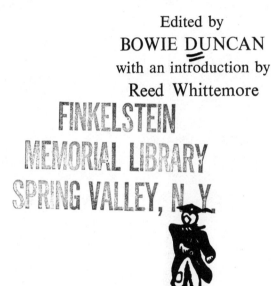

The Scarecrow Press, Inc.
Metuchen, N.J.   1971

72-05313

To Sterett

Contents

Preface

Howard Nemerov is a remarkably accomplished writer who ranges along the gamut of literary forms, expressing himself in the short story, the novel, the drama, the essay, and most notably in poetry. He is also in the tradition of creative writers who are scholars as well, for he seems to lead a life by and for words, in an educational community, leaving his biography on the fly leaf of his books free of a list of experiences on ranches, oil wells, and wheat farms.

He was born on March 1, 1920, and was graduated from Harvard in 1940 with a number of poems and short stories in the Harvard Advocate and the Bourdon Essay Prize to his credit. He joined the R. A. F. upon graduation, transferred to the United States Air Force and was discharged in 1945, having published more poems and short stories in little magazines. After living in New York for a year after the war and completing his first collection of poetry, The Image and the Law, he began his teaching career at Hamilton College, where he also began in earnest his career as a literary critic, associating himself with and contributing extensively to Furioso, the literary magazine he helped edit with his friend, the poet Reed Whittemore. After two years at Hamilton, he moved to Bennington College (1948-1966) and then to Brandeis University where he now teaches. During 1958-1959 he was a visiting lecturer at the University of Minnesota, in 1962-1963 a writer in residence at Hollins College, in 1963-1964 the poet in residence at the Library of

Congress, and during 1969-1970 a writer in residence at Washington University.

He has been acknowledged a major contemporary writer and his awards attest to the quality of his work as well as its diversity, for he has won the Blumenthal Prize for poetry in 1958; the Virginia Quarterly Review Short Story Prize in 1969; the National Institute of Arts and Letters Novel Award in 1961; the Arts Award, Brandeis University, 1963; a Guggenheim in 1968; and the Roethke Memorial Poetry Award in 1968.

Although Mr. Nemerov has been acclaimed by some critics as the most important contemporary American poet, he has suffered since the publication of his first book from a contradictory critical response that does not show signs of abating. The controversy over Mr. Nemerov's first book arranged itself around the problem of the poems' success in communicating a reality or experience whose old categories had broken down, and which the poems undertook to reconstitute. His most recent book of new poems, Blue Swallows, was also received with debate over the poems' success in dealing with several levels of reality, and while Kenneth Burke found the attempt successful, Hayden Carruth did not. Thus, controversy continues over Mr. Nemerov's achievement.

As a member of the American Institute of Arts and Letters, a fellow of the American Academy of Arts and Sciences, and a teacher, Mr. Nemerov might be categorized as an "academic" poet, and those critics who have been his detractors have used the word "academic" pejoratively, taking him to task for writing over-intellectualized, mannered poetry. Such critics have long accused Mr. Nemerov of being cold and therefore unpoetic, of being so intensely concerned with structure and form that his poetry becomes lifeless analysis, not poetic creation. From this perspective, Nemerov's sense of form controls and stifles the reality or experience he seeks to present, reducing his poetry to discourse and the experience it reveals to superficiality.

Those critics who favor his poetry generally seek to discover the aesthetic, the beauty, of such a seeming coldness, revealing the possibilities of an art that is at first glance reflective, not emotional. These critics find that when Mr. Nemerov disciplines emotion through his style, the form or style informs and intensifies the experience he wishes to convey. They find Nemerov's sense of form an organic and vital part of the emotions and experience he conveys. Thus, in this view, Mr. Nemerov's poetry expresses a way of being that is reality or experience intensified and illuminated, not mannered and superficial.

Unable to appreciate a self-reflexive and multi-faceted poetry, his detractors have distorted his achievement. Mr. Nemerov's sense of contradictory tensions in a multi-faceted and reverberating reality, and the poetic strategies and visions he employs to perceive and reveal the essence of such a reality, make him, in the opinion of many, the most important among modern and humane poets writing in America today.

This book presents a sampling of critical essays in an effort to reveal the diversity of Mr. Nemerov's reception, and a bibliography of works by and about him to serve those who wish to make further study of Mr. Nemerov.

In compiling the bibliography and the collection of essays, I have become indebted to many people. In particular, I would like to thank Jackson Bryer of Maryland University for giving generously of his time and knowledge throughout the compilation of the book. In addition to Mr. Reed Whitte-more and the authors who so kindly allowed me to reprint their essays, I am particularly grateful to my editors, who made a rough manuscript into a beautiful book. I am also grateful to Mr. Nemerov, his publishers, Barbara Parrot, Shirley Henn, Dorothy Sutherland, Thomas B. Greenslade, Evelyn G. Lauer, Charles R. Andrews, James Penny, Robert M. Agard, Liz Daniels, Upton Bernice Brady, John Buechler, and Mrs. Francis Woodruff who made available information at their disposal. But I am more pleasantly in debt to my wife, Sterett Kelsey, whose enthusiasm and encouragement were of greater value.

Bowie Duncan

Introduction

Howard Nemerov has a number of poems about monuments or the monumental. Monuments represent, he observes, "the rigid domination of the past over present and future." A selection of critical essays and a bibliography is a sort of monument; certainly it tends to suggest that its subject has become a sort of monument; so the chief purpose of this introduction is to remind readers that Nemerov personally is not at this writing monumental at all. He is more like the antithesis for monuments that he provides in one of his poems called "A Spell Before Winter." He is like running water. In his writings he runs steady and deep, and when he is not writing he can frequently be seen loping briskly through airports, a green bag over his shoulder, on his way to address some college multitude.

Yet the stillness of still things does fascinate him, whether stone or feather. I think of him as more a poet of still lifes than action scenes. Though I don't recall that he has ever done a poem about a bowl of fruit, he could--and if he did, the fruit would speak gravely and eloquently of its ripening-rotting condition. A condition is a state, a moment (at least) of stasis. I think my favorite Nemerov poem is "The Goose Fish," in which a grinning dead fish on a beach speaks to two lovers. What does the fish tell them? They are not sure, but they are mightily impressed with "so finished a comedian," and he becomes "their patriarch," a monument as it were to a condition that they, though in motion, need fear and respect. The poem is a fine instance of how for Nemerov nature does speak, or how, as he might put it, seeing and saying come to the same. And always the seeing and saying evoke a condition, a state--such a state, for instance, as a poem.

Maybe this volume, if put through a computer programmed to summarize Nemerov's extended literary affairs in a dozen words or so, would come forth with: "The seeing-saying mystery of man's relationship with conditions and things. "

Except that the computer wouldn't know what "mystery" meant.

Nemerov does. Nemerov is one of the most profound of contemporary poets, a true explorer of the mystery of the conscious condition. But also, as he might point out, he is an explorer of the conscious non-condition; for consciousness itself moves beyond being, beyond conditionness, and becomes a movement--like running water. Most of his work has to do with this "divided" character of consciousness. I recommend, as a place to begin, his essay "Attentiveness and Obedience, " in a book he edited called Poets on Poetry. I am sure this book will tell you more about that volume.

Reed Whittemore

Part I:

OVERVIEWS OF HOWARD NEMEROV

1.   Genius of the Shore: The Poetry of Howard Nemerov

by Julia Randall

Originally published in The Hollins Critic, Vol. VI, No. 3, June 1969. Reprinted by permission of the author and The Hollins Critic.

Standing and thinking on the shore of the wide world has long been a favorite situation of the poet. With sand between his toes (the atoms of Democritus? Heaven in a grain?), he gazes out to the swaying unsyllabled sea, and back toward his rocky, babel-tongued city. Birds and stars wheel over him; pods and shards, fishbones and bugs turn up under his feet. Clearly, it is all a Great Writing, in which the poet on the shore is a character attempting to read the sentence in which he appears.

Once, writes Nemerov, villainous William of Occam exploded the dream that we could confidently assign the authorship of the Great Writing. And yet science, social science, and philosophy go on confidently assigning. "Nature," they cry; "Man," they cry: "God," they cry--physics in one tongue, theology in another. What Occam in fact pointed out was that what a thing is in itself in no way depends on how we think of it. But it is by thought embodied in language, and by language embodied in institution, that we construct the civilization in which we live, the human world which so often appears to be simply the Self writ large. The poet's job, strangely enough, is to 'unwrite' by going back to the beginning; to make such speech as we have faithful to 'things as

14

they are' rather than to our arrangements of them; to make
language live by confronting things with the 'innocent' mind of
an Adam, by naming them to themselves afresh through the
powers of that mind which is somehow continuous with them.
Nemerov is not alone in observing how many of our languages
are dead.   Since the medieval synthesis

> It's taken that long for the mind
> To waken, yawn, and stretch, to see
> With opened eyes, emptied of speech
> The real world where the spelling mind
> Imposes with its grammar book
> Unreal relations on the blue
> Swallows.

Nemerov, then, does not seek to impose a vision upon
the world so much as to listen to what it says.   He works in
closer relationship with literal meaning than is presently
fashionable; consequently his worst fault (he says so himself)
is sententiousness, but his corresponding virtue is a clarity
whose object is not to diminish the mystery of the world but
to allow it to appear without the interposition of a peculiar
individuality, or of fancy-work or arabesque.   He is, as much
as any modern can be, a romantic poet; he is a religious poet
without religion; a prophet, especially in the polemical and
ironic mode, without portfolio.   When he writes about history,
as Stanley Hyman has said, his theme is "history from the
point of view of the losers. "   Thus when he wants to write
about Moses, he does so from the point of view of Pharoah
after the Red Sea debacle; and instead of writing about
Perseus, he presents the nitwitted predecessors of that hero,
who approached Medusa without a mirror and were turned to
stone.   To judge by his later poems, being turned to stone is
the least agreeable and most probable fate for human beings
and their institutions together.

II

Nemerov's experience of the Great Society is the common one, and his cry the same cry that has been ringing in
our ears since at least Dover Beach. His poems begin in the
personal pain of the 1940 war, and move through the shock
of specifically modern history to the consideration of human
history generally, backward to the Fall and forward again
through its repetitions. "Succession" pictures history as a
furnished room whose former tenant, a priest, has departed
nobody knows where. The apartment does not record his
stay. The present occupant has

> no further wish to follow him
> Where he has gone, for now the room awaits
> The thud of your belongings and your name--
> How easily it will encompass them!
> Behind the door the sycophantic glass
> Already will reflect you in a frame
> That memorizes nothing but its place.

Indifference and rigidity characterize the room; com-
placency or confusion, the roomers. Any red-blooded American boy can buy a passport to the war, a subway ticket to
Suburbia, even an access to the Academy of Fine Ideas. He
can make like Ike, Santa Claus, Don Juan, Professor Publish,
or any number of free-trial examples (and if not satisfied in
20 years, double your hypocrisy back). The monuments of
his aching intellect resemble the stark angularities of Stein-
berg, and the poet can only serve as wry guide to such ruins,
which include, for instance, New York, the "frozen city"; the
statues in the public gardens; the stacks of the university library; the pulpit; the motel; the segregated cemetery; the
packaged meat in the supermarket; the loyalty oath; the Indian-
head nickel, and so on. The dead goose-fish leers up at
lovers on the beach, and the poet reviews his youth:

Accumulating all those years
The blue annuities of silence some called
Wisdom, I heard sunstorms and exploding stars,
The legions screaming in the German wood--
Old violence petrifying where it stood.

The recording artist of this happy scene is the camera, whose "incisive blade" takes "frozen sections": "Maybe a shot of Lenin tombed in glass." For the camera "makes the constant claim that reality is visible," whereas "language asserts it to be secret, invisible, a product of relations rather than things." But if we look before, we see Lot's wife pillared on the plain, and if we look after we see--but like Saul at Endor we forget what we have seen, which was probably the ghost of Norbert Wiener.

Nevertheless, if there are no capital Heroes, there are, as there have always been, Hangers-On to the pain and the puzzle. "The point of faith," reiterated in several poems, "is that you sweat it out," you <u>continue</u>. In one metaphysical poem, the heart is a voracious vacuum cleaner:

The Vacuum

The house is so quiet now
The vacuum cleaner sulks in the corner closet,
Its bag limp as a stopped lung, its mouth
Grinning into the floor, maybe at my
Slovenly life, my dog-dead youth.

I've lived this way long enough,
But when my old woman died her soul
Went into that vacuum cleaner, and I can't bear
To see the bag swell like a belly, eating the dust
And the woolen mice, and begin to howl

Because there is old filth everywhere
She used to crawl, in the corner and under the stair.
I know now how life is cheap as dirt,
And still the hungry, angry heart
Hangs on and howls, biting at air.

It hangs on and howls in stubborn contradiction to the Pleasure Principle:

> There, toward the end, when the left-handed wish
> Is satisfied as it is given up, when the hero
> Endures his cancer and more obstinately than ever
> Grins at the consolations of religion as at a child's
> Frightened pretensions, and when his great courage
> Becomes a wish to die, there appears so obscurely,
> Pathetically, out of the wounded torment and the play,
> A something primitive and appealing, and still
>   dangerous,
> That crawls on bleeding hands and knees over the
>   floor
> Toward him, and whispers as if to confess; again,
>   again.

What all this amounts to, I suppose, is that salt blood
still beats inside the frozen skull: salt blood we inherit, the
freezer we inhabit.   Or to put it another way, freezing is an
illusion, a trick of the temporal camera, a phase of the land
which claims us but not of the sea which makes prior claims.
In a clarifying poem from Mirrors and Windows, the poet
stands "where the railroad bridge/ Divides the river from the
estuary," deciding that he has fallen from the "symboled
world" into the great silence of "reality."   A loon's cry shat-
ters that silence:

> I thought I understood what that cry meant,
> That its contempt was for the form of things,
> Their doctrines, which decayed--the nouns of stone
> And adjectives of glass--not for the verb
> Which surged in power properly eternal
> Against the seawall of the solid world,
> Battering and undermining what it built,
> And whose respeaking was the poet's act,
> Only and always, in whatever time
> Stripped by uncertainty, despair, and ruin,
> Time readying to die, unable to die
> But damned to life again, and the loon's cry.
> And now the sun was sunken in the sea,
> The full moon high, and stars began to shine.

The "verb's" properly eternal urge to creation and destruc-

tion seems to be echoed in the bleeding hero's confession:
again.   The loon's cry recalls the poet to his job of celebrat-
ing the single force.   Perhaps, after all, there is a coherence in the voices of things.

III

It is tempting to mythologize the history of Howard
Nemerov somewhat as follows.   Hero tramps through rocky
wastes, stout Cortez in reverse, having heard tell of mer-
maids singing (he improvises a song for them in the manner
of his grandfather the Pioneer), of a lake isle Innisfree (a
song in the manner of the indomitable peasantry), and of a
colony at Key West where they have ideas of order (he practices orders).   And indeed his songs are the magic which
carry him, undaunted but not undinted, through the perennial
dangers of pilgrimage.

> In place of pain why should I see
> The sunlight on the bleeding wound?
> Or hear the wounded man's outcry
> Bless the Creation with bright sound?
> I stretch myself on joy as on a rack
> And bear the hunch of glory on my back.

On first looking into Nemerov's hunch, we perceive among
other things the family Bible, the collected works of St. Au-
gustine, Shakespeare, and William Blake, plus what appears
to be a Prelude in brown wraps.   In 1948, arrived at a port
called Bennington, Hero has his first view of the sea, recog-
nizes his mission, and attended by winged tutelaries does not
start building an ark or an empire.   Instead he paces the
beach, one ear landward and one ear seaward, and you will
find him there to this day.

This would, of course, be a poem more true than history.   At about the time he went to live in Vermont, Nemerov had outgrown his immediate influences and had found his

own spare and flexible tongue. And his theory of poetry, later embodied in the Poetry and Fiction essays, was developing out of his own practice and his scrupulous and open-minded attention to literature past and present.

Peter Meinke, in his helpful monograph on the poet (University of Minnesota Pamphlets on American Writers, no. 70), sees Nemerov as, from the beginning, a deeply divided man, as evidenced in "the tensions between his romantic and realistic visions, his belief and unbelief, his heart and mind; and in his alternating production of poetry and prose." I think this is true, and that it is as apparent in the later volumes as in the earlier--perhaps even more so, for the division between the serious and the funny (which Nemerov claims are one) come clearer. Two tones of voice, less distinct in the early work, become apparent. One is the ironic flourish: e.g., at the expense of Santa Claus, the "annual saviour of the economy," who "speaks in the parables of the dollar sign:/Suffer the little children to come to Him." The other is a quiet, insistent, but immensely versatile voice, one which can speak songs, sonnets, and sestinas, but perhaps speaks best the loose blank-verse well exemplified in two short plays, Endor and Cain (in The Next Room of the Dream), and in many quotations included in this essay.

Nemerov's fiction (with which I am not here concerned) is basically comic. The curious self-analytical volume, Journal of the Fictive Life, discusses his personal and professional tensions in Freudian terms, but the goose-chase gets nowhere (well, hardly anywhere): "The net of association, for a responsive intelligence, is endless and endlessly intricate; moreover it never will reach a fundamental or anagogical reading that might simplify and make sense of all the others." But the upshot of the Journal is that if psychology cannot ar-

rive at anagoge, poetry may. Poetry may somehow recognize the substance of things under the disguises of culture
and personality: "the thought comes to me that the predica-
ments of my most characteristic and intimate imagery
strangely belong to Shakespeare too, who resolved them by
the magical poetry of his Last Plays. May it happen to me
also one day that the statue shall move and speak, the
drowned child be found, and the unearthly music sing to me."
Individuality is a form which we must suffer. But it contains a secret power to get beyond itself, to be purified
(Joyce would say) out of personal existence. The mortal
man continues, as in the conclusion to the Journal, in the
birth of his son; the poet continues in the larger spirit of
his poems.

It seems to me that Nemerov's 'progress' consists in
a solution to the predicament of his imagery. Bugs, birds,
trees, and running water have been there from the start;
death, war, and the city are there still, but they are less
disturbing for being more acutely seen, distanced, separated
out. Movement and light permeate The Blue Swallows, as
the title indicates. And it is far and away the most significant and least recognized volume of poems of the 60's. Via
deep doubts, deep self-questionings, painful recognitions, and
sere embracings, Nemerov emerges on the shore between
two worlds whose relation is the subject of his most serious
and most moving poetry. He joins there a ghost whose com-
posite face reminds us now of Shelley, now of Coleridge,
now of Jeremiah, now of Arnold or Roethke. It is a hand-
some face that literature fathers-forth. But literature is only the formal cause, as the well-to-do Jewish parents were
the efficient one. The final cause is neither man's inven-
tion nor his own power:

The aim of the poet is to write poems. Poems
are arrangements of language which illuminate a
connection between the inside and outside of things.
The durability of poems, as objects made out of
language which will be around for some time because people experience this illumination and
therefore like reading them, results from the clarity, force, and coherence with which this connection is made, and not from anything else however
laudable, like the holding of strong opinions, or
the feeling of strong emotions, or the naming of
beautiful objects. Because of the oddly intimate
relations obtaining between the inside and the outside of things, the poetic art is always with us,
and does not decay with the decay of systems of
philosophy and religion, or fall out of fashion with
the sets of names, habitually given, over more or
less long periods of time, to the relations between
the inside of things and the outside. With all the
reverence poets have for tradition, poetry is always capable of reaching its beginning again. Its
tradition, ideally, has to do with reaching the beginning, so that, of many young poets who begin
with literature, a few old ones may end up with
nature.

IV

"Wo ist zu diesem Innen/ ein Aussen?" cries Rilke

like a blind man. And Coleridge:

In looking at objects of Nature while I am thinking,
as at yonder moon dim-glimmering through the
dewy window-pane, I seem rather to be seeking,
as it were asking for a symbolical language for
something within me that already and forever
exists.

And Nemerov:

I look not so much at nature as I listen to what it
says. This is a mystery, at least in the sense
that I cannot explain it--why should a phrase come
to you out of the ground and seem to be exactly
right? But the mystery appears to me as the poet's proper relation with things, a relation in
which language, that accumulated wisdom and folly
in which the living and the dead speak simultane-

ously, is a full partner and not merely a stenog-
rapher.

It is odd that we have to learn a language in which to
talk to our central selves, and that the artist should be our
naive tutor; that the eyes turned into the skull are blind until thought illuminates the objects inside as the sun illuminates those outside.   But it is by its likeness to natural or
objective form that we recognize psychic or subjective form,
through the medium of the living art-form.

> The way a word does when
> It senses on one side
> A thing and on the other
> A thought; like sunlight
> On marble, or burnished wood,
> That seems to be coming from
> Within the surface and
> To be one substance with it--
> That is one way of doing
>
> One's being in a world
> Whose being is both thought
> And thing, where neither thing
> Nor thought will do alone
> Till either answers other.

In Creative Intuition in Art and Poetry, Jacques Mari-
tain writes:

> The poet does not know himself in the light of his
> own essence.   Since man perceives himself only
> through a repercussion of his knowledge of the
> world of things, and remains empty to himself if
> he does not fill himself with the universe, the poet
> knows himself only on condition that things resound
> in him, and that in him, at a single wakening,
> they and he come forth together out of sleep.   In
> other words, the primary requirement of poetry,
> which is the obscure knowing, by the poet, of his
> own subjectivity, is inseparable from, is one with
> another requirement--the grasping, by the poet, of
> the objective reality of the outer and inner world;
> not by means of concepts and conceptual knowledge,
> but by means of an obscure knowledge . . . through
> affective union.

That art is an objectification of invisible life in terms
of the visible and sensible world, that is the essential means
to self-awareness not of individual life (I am Jane Doe of
1842 Williamson Road) but of common human life (I am Adam,
I am Hamlet), and that such awareness of life "in widest
commonalty spread" is the best agent of sympathy and hence
of disinterested action--all this Romanticism made apparent.
Nemerov, conscious of the potentiality of romantic or pseudo-
romantic attitudes for self-delusion, and wondering if he is
not sometimes their dupe, is shy of claiming a moral role
for poetry.   Only occasionally, as in his lines to Lu Chi,
does he glance openly at the effect of a purified dialect on
the tribe:

> Neither action nor thought,
> Only the concentration of our speech
> In fineness and in strength (your axe again),
> Till it can carry, in those other minds,
> A nobler action and a purer thought.

He does claim, however, poetry's power to bear new
parts of a world up to consciousness out of an unmindful
"sleep of causes."   One of his figures is the chess-board or
tennis-court: the room of our dream defined by the traditional rules, the "nouns of stone and adjectives of glass."
"The existence of tennis courts is also a guarantee of the
existence of undefined spaces that are not tennis courts, and
where tennis playing is unthinkable.   The object of exploration is to find what is unthinkable in those immensities."   The
object of exploration, Eliot claims, is to arrive where we
started.   Nemerov too implies that the out-of-court immensities may be our being's heart and home; that the poet, if we
attend him, may guide us there.   But he is often in doubt.
If we started in the neat Commercial Gardens, then

              it is right that we return
     To exit where we started, nothing in our hands.

He is certain that wherever we started, it will not be knowledge we carry off in the end. The art-form which imitates
not our appearance (the camera does that) but our living relations, is not a means to conceptual knowledge; it is a light
which illuminates wider and wider areas of our obscure experience, the next and next room of the single dream.

         To watch water, to watch running water
         Is to know a secret, seeing the twisted rope
         Of runnels on the hillside, the small freshets
         Leaping and limping down the tilted field
         In April's light, the green, grave and opaque
         Swirl in the millpond where the current slides
         To be combed and carded silver at the fall;
         It is a secret. Or it is not to know
         The secret, but to have it in your keeping,
         A locked box, Bluebeard's room, the deathless thing
         Which it is death to open. Knowing the secret,
         Keeping the secret--herringbones of light
         Ebbing on beaches, the huge artillery
         Of tides--it is not knowing, it is not keeping,
         But being the secret hidden from yourself.

     The secret which we are is the same as the secret in
the seed, in the sea, in the word. Nothing belongs to the
self alone, although thought belongs to the human mind alone.
And thought, like its parent nature, is fiercely generative,
both of what it sees as good and of what it sees as evil.

         Great pain was in the world before we came.
         The shriek had learned to answer to the claw
         Before we came; the gasp, the sigh, the groan,
         Did not need our invention. But all these
         Immediacies refused to signify
         Till in the morning of the mental sun
         One moment shuddered under stress and broke
         Irreparably into before and after,
         Inventing patience, panic, doubt, despair,
         And with a single thrust producing thought
         Beyond the possible, building the vaults
         Of debt and the high citadels of guilt,
         The segregating walls of obligation,

> All that imposing masonry of time
> Secretly rooted at the earth's cracked hearth,
> In the Vishnu schist and the Bright Angel shale,
> But up aspiring past the visible sky.

Great pain was (and is) in the world; great loveliness, too.
Happiness is "helpless" before the fall of the white waters
(of time) which bear away "this filth" (of personal and communal history).   Nemerov can watch the spring freshets and
speak of the literal rising of the dead.   He can break a stick
and find "nothing that was not wood, nothing/That was not
God."   The stick can figure equally well the tree of Eden or
of Calvary, the forest tree brought down by the vine, the
family tree or its sexual organ, Aaron's rod, Daphne's wrist,
and so on in an endless string of ambiguities which keeps
fraying out and away "since Adam's fall/ Unraveled all."
The poet makes his knot and holds it up to our attention.
But he can't knot water.   He can only tell us

> A new thing: even the water
> Flowing away beneath those birds
> Will fail to reflect their flying forms,
> And the eyes that see become as stones
> Whence never tears shall fall again.

V

Meanwhile, at least the poet "by arts contemplative,"
finds and names reality again.   Like Conrad's Marlow ("my
favorite person in fiction"), he is enamoured of simple
facts but finds the world unavoidably symbolic.   Writing of
Nabokov, Nemerov says

> His subject is always the inner insanity and how it
> may oddly match or fail to match the outer ab-
> surdity, and this problem he sees as susceptible
> only of artistic solutions.   He may well be the ac-
> countant of the universe . . . but he is not its
> moral accountant, and his double entries seek on-
> ly the exact balance between inside and outside,
> self and world, in a realm to which morality

> stands but as a dubious, Euclidean convenience;
> that balance is what in the arts is conventionally
> called <u>truth</u>.

In his excellent book, <u>The Lyrical Novel,</u> Ralph Freedman
writes: "Equating the subject and object of awareness with
the 'inner' and the 'outer', Virginia Woolf suggests that both
are included in a single whole." And Woolf herself writes
of Conrad: "one must be possessed of the double vision; one
must be at once inside and out. To praise . . . silence,
one must possess a voice." So, according to Nemerov,

> the work of art is religious in nature, not because
> it beautifies an ugly world or pretends that a
> naughty world is a nice one--for these things es-
> pecially art does not do--but because it shows of
> its own nature that things drawn within the sacred
> circle of its forms are transfigured, illuminated
> by an inward radiance which amounts to goodness
> because it amounts to Being itself. In the life
> conferred by art, Iago and Desdemona, Edmund
> and Cordelia, the damned and the blessed, equally
> achieve immortality by their relation with the cre-
> ating intelligence which sustains them. The art
> work is not responsible for saying that things in
> reality are so, but rather for revealing what this
> world says to candid vision. It is thus that we
> delight in tragedies whose actions in life would
> merely appall us. And it is thus that art, by its
> illusions, achieves a human analogy to the resolu-
> tion of that famous question of theodicy--the rela-
> tion of an Omnipotent Benevolence to evil--which
> the theologians, bound to the fixed forms of things,
> have for centuries struggled with, intemperately
> and in vain. And it is thus that art, by vision and
> not by dogma, patiently and repeatedly offers the
> substance of things hoped for, the evidence of
> things unseen.

These are high claims, and easily misread. But we cannot
misread two necessary qualities of the poet: openness and
the double vision, qualities which Howard Nemerov possesses
to a high degree. Look inward, look outward, and speak of
what you have seen. But finally, perhaps,

            poems are not
The point.   Finding again the world,
That is the point, where loveliness
Adorns intelligible things
Because the mind's eye lit the sun.

2.   Twenty Years of Accomplishment

by Peter Meinke

Originally published in the Florida Quarterly,
October 1968.   Reported by permission of the
author and the Florida Quarterly.   Copyright
1968 by Peter Meinke.

It's a bad word, perhaps, but Howard Nemerov is really a philosopher.   And judging from the scant space allotted him in the latest books on modern poetry, he is still one of our most underrated poets, despite a steadily widening audience (his New & Selected Poems, for example, is in its fourth printing).   His latest book confirms what really has been evident since 1955 and The Salt Garden: more than any other contemporary poet, Nemerov speaks to the existential, science-oriented (or -displaced), liberal mind of the 20th century.

The Blue Swallows, published exactly 20 years after his first book, is Nemerov's seventh book of poetry, and the 67 new poems it contains represent not so much a culmination of his efforts as another step along a clearly defined technical evolution, and another elucidation (another series of examples) of what might be called a philosophy of minimal affirmation.   Like his gulls and swallows, Nemerov circles around and around the things of this world, finding them insubstantial, frightening, illusory, beautiful, and strange.   Nowhere is his basically pessimistic view of man as both hopeless and indomitable better expressed than in the conclusion

29

of his new poem, "Beyond the Pleasure Principle":

> There, toward the end, when the left-handed wish
> Is satisfied as it is given up, when the hero
> Endures his cancer and more obstinately than ever
> Grins at the consolations of religion as at a child's
> Frightened pretensions, and when his great courage
> Becomes a wish to die, there appears, so obscurely,
> Pathetically, out of the wounded torment and the
>   play,
> A something primitive and appealing, and still
>   dangerous,
> That crawls on bleeding hands and knees over the
>   floor
> Toward him, and whispers as if to confess:
>   <u>again</u>, <u>again</u>.

In Nemerov's first two books, <u>The Image and the Law</u>
(1947) and <u>Guide to the Ruins</u> (1950), the same pessimism is
evident, but without the technical control, the assimilation of
influences. In these early books Nemerov, an ex-RAF pilot,
is "writing the war out of his system," as they say; he is
also, more importantly, writing A) Eliot, B) Yeats, and
C) Stevens out of his system:

> A) Descending and moving closer
>   I saw the sad patience of
>   The people awaiting death
>   (They crossed their bony legs,
>   Their eyes stared, hostile and
>   Bright as broken glass).

> B) But I, except in bed,
>   Wore hair-cloth next the skin,
>   And nursed more than my child
>   That grudge against my side.
>   Now, spirit and flesh assoil'd,
>   I lace my pride in,
>   Crying out odd and even
>   Alas! that ever I did sin,
>   It is fully merry in heaven.

> C) What, Amicus, constitutes mastery?
>   The perdurable fire of a style?

The early poems in general have an abstract, literary qual-

ity, an esoteric vocabulary, many allusions. One marked
tendency in Nemerov's technical development has been a
growing simplicity and directness, not toward the "country"
simplicity of Robert Frost, but the simplicity of a highly
educated man trying to convey the substance of his meditations clearly.

Critics often note in his earlier work the influence of
Auden. While one can find it in an occasional flatness of
tone, Nemerov's wit is his own. (In the same way his novels have been compared to Evelyn Waugh's, but both of these
similarities are only real insofar as wit is similar to wit.)
Wit is certainly a constant element in Nemerov's work:
puns, irony, satire, epigrams, jokes; these are not extrusive
from his main body of poetry, but integral to it. Nemerov
has said, "The serious and the funny are one." This is
even more true of The Blue Swallows than of his earlier
books.

The other main element besides wit that is carried
over from his early poetry is a concern with theological
questions, reflected often in Biblical subject matter (e.g.,
his two verse plays, "Cain" and "Endor"), but more often
in a running dialogue with Christianity. Nemerov's own religious position seems to be that of a non-practicing Jew who
is constantly wrestling with the problem of faith. An early
sonnet ends: "The question is of science not to doubt / The
point of faith is that you sweat it out." This is still an important theme in his latest book (e.g., "Creation of Anguish,"
"Cybernetics").

It was in his third book, The Salt Garden, that Nemerov first pulled together his talent and intelligence; originally a "city" poet, Nemerov moved to Bennington, Vermont, in
1948; and nature has been a unifying element in his work

since The Salt Garden (in 1967 he was given the $1000 St.
Botolph Club Arts Award for "a poet of accomplishment and
promise, native to, or primarily associated with, New England). "The Goose Fish," "The Pond," "I Only Am Escaped Alone to Tell Thee," "The Salt Garden," are just a
few of the poems from The Salt Garden which have become
familiar to readers of contemporary poetry.

Also in The Salt Garden the two main influences on
Nemerov emerge. His subjects and the flexible rhythms of
his meditative blank verse reflect a close study of Wordsworth and Frost: he is one of the few poets to really learn
from these masters:

> Line, leaf, and light; darkness invades our day;
> No meaning in it, but indifference
> Which does not flatter with profundity.
> Nor is it drama. Even the giant oak,
> Stricken a hundred years ago or yesterday,
> Has not found room to fall as heroes should . . .

The typical adjective used to describe nature is "brutal,"
and the link between brutal nature and "decent" bumbling man
is found in the liquids, ocean and blood, which fuse into
man's "salt dream," the submerged and subconscious call of
the wild. And while Nemerov's lyrical intelligent voice
brooding over nature and man dominates this book, there is
also great variety of tone and subject: e.g., the telescoped
images of "I Only Have Escaped Alone to Tell Thee," the
surreal dream sequence "The Scales of the Eyes."

The trend toward nature begun in The Salt Garden continues in Mirrors & Windows (1958), the difference being
that in the latter book Nemerov is consciously aware that he
is a poet looking at nature, trying to capture it in his poems: "Study this rhythm, not this thing. /The brush's tip
streams from the wrist/of a living man, a dying man. /The

mirror

running water is the wrist."

"A Day on the Big Branch" is a good example of
Nemerov's attitude, which might be called realistic romanticism.   That is, the poems seem to be composed by a romantic sensibility which is at the same time too analytical
and honest to see things other than as they are.   Nemerov's
rocks are "hard as rocks" and when the half-drunk card
players climb into the wilderness nothing very glorious hap-
pens--except that as they talk of the war and of life, the ma-
jestic beauty of nature forces them into "poetry and truth:"

> so that at last one said, "I shall play cards
> until the day I die," and another said,
> "in bourbon whiskey are all the vitamins
> and minerals needed to sustain man's life,"
> and still another, "I shall live on smoke
> until my spirit has been cured of flesh."

Another outstanding poem of minimal affirmation is "The
Town Dump," a savage metaphor for civilization (in Nemerov's novels the pessimism is redeemed by the humor; generally speaking, in Nemerov's poetry the pessimism is redeemed by beauty, often symbolized by birds):

> . . . . You may sum up
> The results, if you want results. But I will add
> That wild birds, drawn to the carrion and flies,
> Assemble in some numbers here, their wings
> Shining with light, their flight enviably free,
> Their music marvelous, though sad, and strange.

Mirrors & Windows often reminds one of Hart Crane's lines
which Nemerov used as an epigraph for his novel, Federigo:
"As silent as a mirror is believed / Realities plunge in silence by . . ."   The object of poetry is to catch as in a
mirror the beauty and terror of life, not to make life pret-
tier, not to make it easier for us, not even to help us understand it.   "Some shapes cannot be seen in a glass, /
those are the ones the heart breaks at."   The poems in this

book are life-reflecting mirrors, and windows through which
we see with the poet's "infinitely penetrant" eye. Nemerov's
poetry has become considerably more visual:

> It was as promised, a wonder, with granite walls
> enclosing ledges, long and flat, of limestone,
> or, rolling, of lava; within the ledges
> the water, fast and still, pouring its yellow light,
> and green, over the tilted slabs of the floor,
> blackened at shady corners, falling in a foam
> of crystal to a calm where the waterlight
> dappled the ledges as they leaned
> against the sun; big blue dragonflies hovered
> and darted and dipped a wing, hovered again
> against the low wind moving over the stream,
> and shook the flakes of light from their clear wings.

New & Selected Poems (1960) contains only fifteen new poems; the new note is an overriding concern with his "deare
times waste." Time and the loss of innocence, of friends,
of hope, are the themes: "I cried because life is hopeless
and beautiful," he writes, and the beauty teaches him to "endure and grow." The central poem--Nemerov's longest--is
"Runes," symmetrically consisting of fifteen-line stanzas (a
stanza form very suitable to his talent, e.g., "The Beekeeper Speaks" in The Blue Swallows). Like "The Scales of
the Eyes," "Runes" is a sort of dream sequence, but more
tightly organized, the fifteen stanzas being meditations clust-
ered around the images of water and seed, "Where time to
come has tensed / Itself." The smooth run-on blank verse
lines match rhythm and content:

> Consider how the seed lost by a bird
> Will harbor in its branches most remote
> Descendants of the bird; while everywhere
> And unobserved, the soft green stalks and tubes
> Of water are hardening into wood, whose hide,
> Gnarled, knotted, flowing, and its hidden grain,
> Remember how the water is streaming still.
> Now does the seed asleep, as in a dream
> Where time is compacted under pressures of

> Another order, crack open like stone
> From whose division pours a stream, between
> The raindrop and the sea, running in one
> Direction, down, and gathering in its course
> That bitter salt which spices us the food
> We sweat for, and the blood and tears we shed.

The water streaming in the seed streams through our world,
our bodies, holding everything together in its always-chang-
ing permanence. The subtle rhythms support the imagery in
a fusion of form and content; run-ons, alliteration, repetition, all playing important roles in the structure. The "s"
sound in "soft green stalks and tubes," the "d" sound in
"hardening into wood, whose hide, / Gnarled, knotted" rein-
force the meaning; the rhythm, stopped by "whose hide, /
Gnarled, knotted," flows forward again with "Flowing, and
its hidden grain." The end of the first sentence holds the
paradox of permanent impermanence in the ambiguous
"streaming still." The onomatopoeic "crack" splits the second sentence, whose alliteration and longer phrases ("gather-
ing in its course / That bigger salt which spices us the food
/ We sweat for") underline the stanza's conclusion.

Nemerov's sixth book of poems, The Next Room of
the Dream (1962), continues his trend toward a more simple
and clear verse, emphasizing natural description: "Now I
can see certain simplicities / In the darkening rust and tarnish of the time, / And say over the certain simplicities, /
The running water and the standing stone . . ." And yet,
as he writes in another poem, "Nothing will yield:" art
smashes on the rocks of reality. Often attacked for being
too "cold" or "cerebral," Nemerov's poetry is actually quite
the opposite: a passion disciplined, but passionate and hu-
manitarian nevertheless, with cries of anguish constantly
breaking through: "--Nothing can stand it!" Poems like

"Lion & Honeycomb" and "Vermeer" express his ars poetica,
his striving for rhythms "Perfected and casual as to a child's
eye / Soap bubbles are, and skipping stones"; poems like
"The Iron Characters" and "Somewhere" express his humani-
tarianism; poems like "To Clio, Muse of History" and "The
Dial Tone" are metaphysical expressions of his belief in the
unreality of reality, the reality of the void.

The Blue Swallows is a worthy successor to these
books.   Divided into four sections, it has the variety, wit,
and technical skill we have come to expect; it is also full of
wisdom and gentleness:

> . . . even the water
> Flowing away beneath those birds
> Will fail to reflect their flying forms,
> And the eyes that see become as stones
> Whence never tears shall fall again.
>
> O swallows, swallows, poems are not
> The point.   Finding again the world,
> That is the point, where loveliness
> Adorns intelligible things
> Because the mind's eye lit the sun.

While the themes and images are often specifically contemporary (Auschwitz, burning monks, a Negro cemetery, cybernetics), Nemerov is mainly concerned with finding timeless
metaphors for the human condition, "relation's spindrift web."
In poem after poem we are likened (without his saying so explicitly) to cherries picked off trees, snowflakes falling in
black water, lobsters waiting in a tank, days falling into
darkness, planted rows dwindling to wilderness, fields becoming shadow.   These poems are used more or less con-
trapuntally with tremendously effective satire on The Great
Society ("Money," "On the Platform," "To the Governor &
Legislature of Massachusetts").   A typical example (not best,
but chosen for brevity) is "Keeping Informed in D. C. :"

Each morning when I break my buttered toast
Across the columns of the Morning Post,
I am astounded by the ways in which
Mankind has managed once again to bitch
Things up to a degree that yesterday
Had looked impossible.   Not far away
From dreams of mind, I read this dream of theirs,
And think: It's true, we are the bankrupt heirs
Of all the ages, history is the bunk.
If you do not believe in all this junk,
If you're not glad things are not as they are,
      You can wipe your arse on the Evening Star.

Nature, still treated unromantically, permeates these poems; in "The Companions," which is a sort of modern "Immortality Ode," Nemerov describes the pull towards nature that, for example, Frost writes about in "Directive." But Nemerov refuses to see "messages" there: "That's but interpretation, the deep folly of man / To think that things can squeak at him more than things can." A fascination with light, "Firelight in sunlight, silver pale," also plays over these pages, and indeed these poems can be thought of as the "small flames" which conclude the book's final poem:

So warm, so clear at the line of corded velvet
The marvelous flesh, its faster rise and fall,
Sigh in the throat, the mouth fallen open,
The knees fallen open, the heavy flag of the skirt
Urgently gathered together, quick, so quick,
Black lacquer, bronze, blue velvet, gleam
Of pewter in a tarnishing light, the book
Of the body lying open at the last leaf,
Where the spirit and the bride say, Come,
As from deep mirrors on the hinted wall
Beyond these shadows, a small flame sprouts.

One reason that Nemerov speaks to this age is that his poetry attempts to come to terms with science: not just psychology (in which Nemerov is well versed, vide his Journal of the Fictive Life), but "hard" science. Light years and nebulae, the speed of light, electrodes, a heterodyne hum, physicists and particles, are typical subjects for him.

His general position seems to be that science is "true," but
never quite accounts for our lives (though it tries): science
lacks "blood" and "mystery;" it misses the essential:

> For "nothing in the universe can travel at the speed
> Of light," they say, forgetful of the shadow's speed.

While Nemerov's typical form is the loose blank verse
line, in The Blue Shadows he uses more short-lined poems,
trimeter and dimeter, than in his earlier work, keeping with
his trend toward simplicity. In this form, too, his rhythms
are varied and subtle, as in the first stanza of "Celestial
Globe:"

> This is the world
> Without the world.
> I hold it in my hand
> A hollow sphere
> Of childlike blue
> With magnitudes of stars.
> There in its utter dark
> The singing planets go,
> And the sun, great source,
> Is blazing forth his fires
> Over the many-oceaned
> And river-shining earth
> Whereon I stand
> Balancing the ball
> Upon my hand.

To sum up. The Blue Swallows is the work of a poet who is a master of his craft; rhythm, image, sound fuse
in poem after poem. And the poetry speaks to us, as poems should. There is no certainty, much agony, our minds
bow down "Among the shadows / Of shadowy things, / Itself
a shadow / Less sure than they." Nemerov's general intelligence and craftsmanship perhaps seem old-fashioned today,
when blood-and-guts, a confessional softness, and a sort of
sloppiness are thought to be more "honest" or "spontane-
ous;" he is perhaps closer in spirit to, say, Pope, who is
also out of favor (nevertheless the 18th century is called the

Age of Pope).   And underneath the darkness Nemerov contin-
ally strikes the existential spark, as in the conclusion of his
poem describing an oil slick polluting a stream:

> The curve and glitter of it as it goes
> The maze of its pursuit, reflect the water
> In agony under the alien, brilliant skin
> It struggles to throw off and finally does
> Throw off, on its frivolous purgatorial fall
> Down to the sea and away, dancing and singing
> Perpetual intercession for this filth--
> Leaping and dancing and singing, forgiving everything.

3.   A Prophet Armed

by Robert D. Harvey

> Originally published in Poets in Progress,
> edited by H. B. Hungerford. (Chicago:
> Northwestern University Press, 1967).
> Reprinted by permission of Northwestern
> University Press.

Howard Nemerov has referred to himself as a "writer
of fictions in verse and in prose," and in evidence for the
assertion has published since 1947 three novels, a book of
short stories, and five volumes of verse.   The last of these,
New and Selected Poems (1960), offers fifteen new poems
(one of which, "Runes," is itself a cycle of fifteen lyrics),
together with about forty poems from earlier collections.
A few of these are from the early volumes, The Image and
the Law (1947) and Guide to the Ruins (1950), but the bulk of
them are divided equally between The Salt Garden (1955) and
Mirrors & Windows (1958).   Published as the poet reached
the decisive age of forty, New and Selected Poems provides
a solid retrospective exhibition of Mr. Nemerov's accomplishment in verse.

Nemerov's novels are light, well-plotted comedies,
full of pell-mell wit.   They are brilliant, epigrammatic satires upon contemporary American life.   His fiction shows
him as a man of reason who knows very well how to reveal
his moral passion beneath a mask of comic satire.   His poetry is another matter--but not wholly other.   It is easy to

sense in the poems the value of his novelist's experience; one recalls Pound's crafty advice that poets try to write verse as good as good prose. The man is far more thoroughly committed in his verse; but in drawing upon the deeper levels of his imagination for his poems, Nemerov does not refuse his wit fair room for play. He composes epigrams and satires as well as serious lyrics, and the instance has arisen when the reviewer has trouble telling one from the other. In his more fully realized work the wit becomes, like miner's dynamite, an energetic and disciplined tool. The verse of the last few years--the verse of New and Selected Poems--amply demonstrates his capacity for integrating complex materials by means of a mature and powerful technical equipment of diction, imagery, and rhythm.

Nemerov was born and reared in New York City and graduated from Harvard (1941) just in time for the war. He joined the RCAF, trained in Canada and England, and then in American uniform flew with a RAF squadron over the North Sea in strikes against Nazi shipping. After the spell of violence he returned with an English wife to a quiet life of teaching and writing. He has been a member of the literature faculty at Bennington College since 1948. The three important experiences seem to have been the city childhood, the wartime violence, and the impact after these of nature-- the sea and the Vermont hills. Nemerov's imagination has taken city, war, and nature, and shaped from them a complex and compelling world.

The early poem, "Redeployment,"[1] which he reprinted in the new volume, is a good introduction to the theme of war:

> They say the war is over. But water still
> Comes bloody from the taps, and my pet cat

In his disorder vomits worms which crawl
Swiftly away.   Maybe they leave the house.
These worms are white, and flecked with the
        cat's blood.

The war may be over.   I know a man
Who keeps a pleasant souvenir, he keeps
A soldier's dead blue eyeballs that he found
Somewhere--hard as chalk, and blue as slate.
He clicks them in his pocket while he talks.

And now there are cockroaches in the house,
They get slightly drunk on DDT,
Are hard, fast, shifty--can be drowned but not
Without you hold them under quite some time.
People say the Mexican kind can fly.

The end of the war.   I took it quietly
Enough.   I tried to wash the dirt out of
My hair and from under my fingernails,
I dressed in clean white clothes and went to bed.
I heard the dust falling between the walls.

The protagonist protests too much: Nemerov's irony depends
upon that insistent reiteration.   For of course the point is
that the war is not over.   The hysterical violence of the imagery imparts a nightmarish quality.   We shall see the poet
making more use of this surrealist technique in later poems.
The nightmare is in familiar enough surroundings--cheap
metropolitan lodgings are suggested--there is even an air of
domesticity: the faucet, the cat, the cockroaches, the per-
vading dirt; we have no trouble recognizing this "unreal
city."   The protagonist may have nowhere to go, but he
bathes and dresses to go sleepless to bed, alone and alert to
hear the silence of the dust falling.   He insanely accepts
these horrors as a matter of course: "the water still comes
bloody"; the cockroaches, yes, are a nuisance, but means
are being worked out to deal with them--imperfect means, to
be sure; the pet cat "in his disorder" vomits horribly, but
the worms "crawl swiftly away," and "maybe they leave the

house." The air of the tentative here suggests the similar
horror of Kafka, as does also the random incuriosity about
that place where the protagonist's friend has found those eyeballs. Throughout, Nemerov manages this juxtaposition of
the ordinary and the monstrous or obscene with considerable
distinction. He slips perhaps in the brashness of "pleasant
souvenir." But that "but not without you hold them," is a
fine touch of dialect.

"The Soldier Who Lived Through the War" is the title
of another early piece. Whether this means simply that the
soldier has survived, or that he has really lived only in the
commitment to violence (both meanings are there), the result is the same: the "war" continues. Life is seen, after
the experience of war, as either dangerous and contingent
and vital, or a vacant drift to nothingness. Questioning the
danger, for a poet, of a career in teaching, Nemerov once
remarked, "I have seen dangers in the academic life, but so
are there dangers everywhere." This view persists, and in
a new poem, "Life Cycle of Common Man," the poet flatly
calculates the number of cigarettes and whiskey empties,
"bones, broken shoes, frayed collars and worn out or outgrown diapers and dinner-jackets" an ordinary man strews in
his wake, then demands that we

> Consider the courage in all that, and behold the man
> Walking into deep silence, with the ectoplastic
> Cartoon's balloon of speech proceeding
> Steadily out of the front of his face, the words
> Borne along on the breath which is his spirit
> Telling the numberless tale of his untold Word
> Which makes the world his apple, and forces
>   him to eat.

The war is not over. The dangers of commitment to the
chaos of "reality" are the same everywhere, but facing these
dangers, accepting the commitment, is what constitutes life;

the only ultimate danger is to refuse the commitment, to
stop "walking into the deep silence"; that refusal, that stop-
page, is death.

The thematic differences between the early "Redeployment" and the new "Life Cycle of Common Man" may be
summed up in the difference between hysterical paralysis and
stoical courage.   The shabby horror of death becomes the
grotesque and comic absurdity of life; nightmare isolation
gives way to man walking and talking--Joyce's Stephen Deda-
lus, that narcissistic young madman, to fortyish, wife-foolish
but fatherly wise Leopold Bloom.

Nemerov himself has remarked that he was a "city
boy who came late to the country; 'nature,' whatever that is,
had a powerful effect for being an effect so long delayed."
I have said that Nemerov composes his imaginative world out
of war, city, and nature.   In his later verse he uses the war
theme to express the endless struggle between city and nature, between mind and world.   The title poem of his third
volume (1955), "The Salt Garden," presents a concrete image
in which the depth of his city-nature complex can begin to be
gauged.   A man having "with an amateur's toil" and "much
patience, and some sweat" made a pleasant greenery

> From a difficult, shallow soil
> That, now inland, was once the shore
> And once, maybe, the ocean floor,

watches his place "bend in the salt wind," and becomes suddenly aware of the mighty though distant ocean.   Despising
for the moment his puny achievement and so made restless,
he rises at dawn and encounters "a great gull come from the
mist."   The gull "stared upon my green concerns" like a
"merchant prince come to some poor province," then "fought
his huge freight into air and vanished seaward with a cry."

The poem concludes:

> When he was gone
> I turned back to the house
> And thought of wife, of child,
> And of my garden and my lawn
> Serene in the wet dawn;
> And thought that image of the wild
> Wave where it beats the air
> Had come, brutal, mysterious,
> To teach the tenant gardener,
> Green fellow of this paradise
> Where his salt dreams lie.

There is a suggestion of Yeats' wild swans in this.   But Nemerov's distinct stamp is upon it.   What emerges for the city man's awareness from his encounter with the great gull is an inexplicable sense of identity with the bird.   Men build cities and so become human.   But in becoming human they enter upon the hazards of the moral life.   In emerging from and building ramparts against " 'nature,' whatever that is," they lose their innocence--in a word, they "fall."   Nemerov draws a good deal upon the Old Testament, and he is aware that both Jerusalem and Babylon were cities--and so was Sodom.   And so was Nagasaki.   In reclaiming a bit of what was "once the shore and once, maybe, the ocean floor," this amateur naturalist from the city is bringing his limited human skill in contact with the great reservoir from which that very skill--his human consciousness--appears to separate him.   That separation constitutes the fall of man; that contact, his salvation.   The feeling of helplessness, of nonentity, while seen to be invalid as a total response to the encounter, is not wholly denied by the poem's resolution. Man's garden is sowed with salt; his only hope, and that a limited one, is in his own effort that makes it anyhow green.

The meanings contained in these symbols cannot be wholly rendered discursively.   They are symbols, and out

of them the poet is making poems. We can, however, try
to indicate how the three basic areas of Nemerov's imagination which I have abstracted from his verse--city, nature,
and war--are related, and how in the last few years he has
been forcing them to contain at once a broader and deeper
range of meanings.

The theme of war develops an ambivalence: its violence kills, maims, destroys; but its violence is also a form
of energy, of action, of life. The horror of death--whether
physical death or death of the heart or of imagination--is
real enough, and it tends to breed more death, to effect a
paralysis. To grant that reality, but to face it and endure
it, is to find one's identity in terms of the war which produces it. The horror is then strangely transmuted. The
war then reveals itself as the inescapable war of the city
with nature. It is the action of flinging meaning into the
void. It is the experience of committing one's poor human
consciousness, one's more or less skilled battalions of intelligence, against the brute forces of nature, whether without
or within: for the salt sea flows in our veins. It is the
ever-circulating bloodstream whose reverberations we mistake for the sea's surf when we hold the shell to the ear.
Only out of the mind's active struggle to order matter can
the awareness of a larger reality, containing both mind and
matter, emerge. Possessed of such awareness, the poet
renders it in poems.

The meanings here suggested may be illustrated quite
clearly in a fairly long poem from Mirrors & Windows, entitled "The Town Dump." To this poem Nemerov appends an
epigraph from King Lear, which pungently reflects upon the
war of freedom with necessity:

"The art of our necessities is strange,
That can make vile things precious."

A mile out in the marshes, under a sky
Which seems to be always going away
In a hurry, on that Venetian land threaded
With hidden canals, you will find the city
Which seconds ours (so cemeteries, too,
Reflect a town from hillsides out of town),
Where Being most Becomingly ends up
Becoming some more.   From cardboard tenements,
Windowed with cellophane, or simply tenting
In paper bags, the angry mackerel eyes
Glare at you out of stove-in, sunken heads
Far from the sea; the lobster, also, lifts
An empty claw in his most minatory
Of gestures; oyster, crab, and mussel shells
Lie here in heaps, savage as money hurled
Away at the gate of hell.   If you want results,
These are results.
            Objects of value or virtue,
However, are also to be picked up here,
Though rarely, lying with bones and rotten meat,
Eggshells and mouldy bread, banana peels
No one will skid on, apple cores that caused
Neither the fall of man nor a theory
Of gravitation.   People do throw out
The family pearls by accident, sometimes,
Not often; I've known dealers in antiques
To prowl this place by night, with flashlights, on
The off-chance of somebody's having left
Derelict chairs which will turn out to be
By Hepplewhite, a perfect set of six
Going to show, I guess, that in any sty
Someone's heaven may open and shower down
Riches responsive to the right dream; though
It is a small chance, certainly, that sends
The ghostly dealer, heavy with fly-netting
Over his head, across these hills in darkness,
Stumbling in cut-glass goblets, lacquered cups,
And other products of his dreamy midden
Penciled with light and guarded by the flies.

For there are flies, of course.   A dynamo
Composed, by thousands, of our ancient black
Retainers, hums here day and night, steady
As someone telling beads, the hum becoming

A high whine at any disturbance; then,
Settled again, they shine under the sun
Like oil-drops, or are invisible as night,
By night.
       All this continually smoulders,
Crackles, and smokes with mostly invisible fires
Which, working deep, rarely flash out and flare,
And never finish. Nothing finishes;
The flies, feeling the heat, keep on the move.

Among the flies, the purifying fires,
The hunters by night, acquainted with the art
Of our necessities, and the new deposits
That each day wastes with treasure, you may say
There should be ratios. You may sum up
The results, if you want results. But I will add
That wild birds, drawn to the carrion and flies,
Assemble in some numbers here, their wings
Shining with light, their flight enviably free,
Their music marvelous, though sad, and strange.

The dump is the city, returning to " 'nature,' whatever that
is"--just as the cemetery is a city whose inhabitants are returning to nature. The dump is not Mr. Eliot's wasteland,
from which God has turned away; it is rather itself God's
country, or at least a necessary part of it, and if it looks
like Hell, it is indisputably ours. Like the trail of debris
in "Life Cycle of Common Man" it is our past--it is history. One recalls the savage pride of Trotsky's triumphant
taunt, flung at the departing Mensheviks in the Petrograd
Soviet in 1917, "You are all on the ash-heap of history."
It is a Hell, but Gehenna as a matter of fact was Jerusalem's town dump. To conclude that what looks like Hell is
Hell only is to conclude too easily and too soon; "nothing
finishes." Any "ratio" will only sum up the results, "if
you want results": Nemerov contents himself with simply
adding that the marvel of the birds, too, is part of the
ghastly whole.

      In a note to this writer, Mr. Nemerov offered an illuminating off-the-cuff statement:

> Poetry is a kind of spiritual exercise, a (generally doomed but stoical) attempt to pray one's humanity back into the universe; and conversely an attempt to read, to derive anew, one's humanity from nature, nature considered as a book, dictionary and bible at once. Poetry is a doctrine of signatures, or presupposes that the universe is such a doctrine whether well written or ill . . . Poetry is an art of combination, or discovering the secret valencies which the most widely differing things have for one another. In the darkness of this search, patience and good humor are useful qualities. Also: The serious and the funny are one. The purpose of poetry is to persuade, fool, or compel God into speaking.

"Poetry is a doctrine of signatures . . ." In his best work Nemerov presents adumbrations, not a "ratio"; "signatures rather than the Name Itself."

The style of "The Town Dump" is characteristic. In his earlier verse Nemerov was severely criticized for his undisciplined verbal wit. But here the verbal play seems masterfully controlled. "Where Being most Becomingly ends up Becoming some more" is wittily abstract, and the abrupt descent into those raw particulars, rising to "savage as money hurled away at the gate of Hell" expresses a magnificent rage. The flat emptiness of "If you want results, these are results," provides exactly the inane anti-climax he wants. "The serious and funny are one"--a dangerous truth. But the poet seems to me to mix his tonal qualities in this poem in a fully disciplined way. The hysterical soar and swoop of the tonal rhythms correspond exactly to that sustained dynamo hum rising fitfully to a high whine, or that continual smoulder which rarely flashes out and flares.

Nemerov's increasing mastery of his rhythms may be further illustrated by "Trees," also from the 1958 volume.

There is a quiet firmness about this fine sentence, which
constitutes the entire poem:

> To be a giant and keep quiet about it,
> To stay in one's own place;
> To stand for the constant presence of process
> And always to seem the same;
> To be steady as a rock and always trembling,
> Having the hard appearance of death
> With the soft, fluent nature of growth,
> One's Being deceptively armored,
> One's Becoming deceptively vulnerable;
> To be so tough, and take the light so well,
> Freely providing forbidden knowledge
> Of so many things about heaven and earth
> For which we should otherwise have no word--
> Poems or people are rarely so lovely,
> And even when they have great qualities
> They tend to tell you rather than exemplify
> What they believe themselves to be about,
> While from the moving silence of trees,
> Whether in storm or calm, in leaf and naked,
> Night or day, we draw conclusions of our own,
> Sustaining and unnoticed as our breath,
> And perilous also--though there has never been
> A critical tree--about the nature of things.

In this and in a number of other poems from the 1958 volume ("The Map-Maker on His Art," "To Lu Chi," "Writing," "Painting a Mountain Stream," and others), and in the
new poems of the 1960 volume the sonnet-sequence "Runes,"
Nemerov develops his concern with the nature and problems
of poetry or of art in general. He never fails to insist upon the proximate character of art. It is a "generally
doomed but stoical attempt," and when it seems to succeed,
miraculous. In "Writing," for instance, he discovers an in-
telligibility both in Chinese characters and in the scorings of
skaters in ice; both in some way "do world and spirit wed";
both seem to establish a connection between the mind and ex-
ternal reality--indeed, to leave a trace of mind out there.
But he concludes:

        continental faults are not
    bare convoluted fissures in the brain.
    Not only must the skaters soon go home;
    also the hard inscription of their skates
    is scored across the open water, which long
    remembers nothing, neither wind nor wake.

In "Painting a Mountain Stream" he puts aside the pentameter line, whose resources he has explored most fully in his
later verse, and shifts the thematic emphasis as well.
"Running and standing still at once is the whole truth," he
begins, and exhorts the painter to "study this rhythm, not
this thing" in his effort to paint the stream:

        The brush's tip streams from the wrist
        of a living man, a dying man.
        The running water is the wrist.

        In the confluence of the wrist
        things and ideas ripple together . . .

        The water that seemed to stand is gone.
        The water that seemed to run is here.
        Steady the wrist, steady the eye;
        paint this rhythm, not this thing.

Here both the mystery of life--of how things can have, or
be, a rhythm, and the mystery of art--of how man can create things which seem to have, or become, a rhythm, are
presented in curious relationship to each other, for the
painter himself is a rhythm and not a thing, in more ways
than one. In these stanzas Nemerov makes impressive use
of a quiet variation which at once supports and contains his
themes.

        Of course the act of the artist is par excellence ex-
pressive of the war of city and nature, since it most directly reveals the difficulty and mystery of mind or spirit penetrating or even perceiving brute matter. In a number of poems such as "Brainstorm," "Sanctuary," and "Truth," the
essential irrationality of the attempt to be rational is pre-

sented.   To be rational is to attempt to conform the world
to the mind, to reduce William James's "blooming, buzzing
confusion" to a logic.   But if the mind itself be revealed as
part of that blooming and buzzing?   In "Brainstorm" something like that is revealed step by step as a man sitting a-
lone in an upstairs room is distracted from his book first by
the rising wind and then by the crows whose "horny feet so
near but out of sight scratched on the slate" of the roof
overhead.   He speculates, as the windows rattle and the tim-
bers groan in the wind, that house and crows are talking to
each other.

> The secret might be out:
> Houses are only trees stretched on the rack.
> And once the crows knew, all nature would know.

And this leads him to wonder in turn what's to prevent nature, not paradoxically endowed with mind, to invade his ar-
tificially ordered world.   The poem then gallops to a nightmarish conclusion:

> He came to feel the crows walk on his head
> As if he were the house, their crooked feet
> Scratched, through the hair, his scalp.   He might
>   might be dead,
> It seemed, and all the noises underneath
> Be but the cooling of the sinews, veins,
> Juices, and sodden sacks suddenly let go;
> While in his ruins of wiring, his burst mains,
> The rainy wind had been set free to blow
> Until the green uprising and mob rule
> That ran the world had taken over him,
> Split him like seed, and set him in the school
> Where any crutch can learn to be a limb.

> Inside his head he heard the stormy crows.

"The serious and the funny are one"; Nemerov has in
this purged away the jarring shrillness of his early use of
the nightmare.   The rhythm's rush is thoroughly under control.   He handles that dreamlike imagery with ease under

a compression that seems to leave no room at all for ma-
neuver.

A word ought to be said of Nemerov's satirical verse.
It depends upon the same use of the world, but with the difference that the poet chooses to indulge his anger rather
than attempt to find through it a larger integration. Here
is an early example, entitled "On a Text: Jonah IV, xi"--
but first let us quote Scripture. God is remonstrating with
Jonah, who is angry that sinful Nineveh is being spared:
"And should I not spare Nineveh, that great city, wherein
are more than sixscore thousand persons that cannot discern
between their right hand and their left hand; and also much
cattle?" Now Nemerov's verse:

> The Lord might have spared us the harsh joke;
> Many that live in Nineveh these days
> Cannot discern their ass from a hot rock.
> Perhaps the word "cattle" refers to these?

In one of his new poems, Nemerov comments wryly and at
greater length upon a singularly vulnerable remark culled
from the Associated Press, datelined Atlantic City, June 23,
1957. The dispatch, headed "SEES BOOM IN RELIGION,
TOO," reads, in part: "These fruits of material progress,'
said the Rev. Edward L. R. Elson of the National Presby-
terian Church, Washington, 'have provided the leisure, the
energy, and the means for a level of human and spiritual
values never before reached,' " The poem, entitled "Boom!"
begins this way:

> Here at the Vespasian-Carlton, it's just one
> religious activity after another; the sky
> is constantly being crossed by cruciform
> airplanes, in which nobody disbelieves
> for a second . . .

After a quick look at Job, Damien, St. Francis, and Dante,
the poem returns to the charge:

But now the gears mesh and the tires burn
and the ice chatters in the shaker and the priest
in the pulpit, and Thy name, O Lord,
is kept before the public, while the fruits
ripen and religion booms and the level rises
and every modern convenience runneth over,
that it may never be with us as it hath been
with Athens and Karnak and Nagasaki,
nor Thy sun for one instant refrain from shining
on the rainbow Buick by the breezeway
or the Chris Craft with the uplift life raft;
that we may continue to be the just folks we are,
plain people with ordinary superliners and
disposable diaperliners, people of the stop'n'shop
'n'pray as you go, of hotel, motel, boatel,
the humble pilgrims of no deposit no return
and please adjust thy clothing, who will give to
    Thee,
if Thee will keep us going, our annual
Miss Universe, for Thy Name's Sake, Amen.

The details have their satirical bite, but the heavy rhetorical impact depends on their being piled high and at accel-
erated speed. We have seen this device at work in "Brainstorm." The fire of Nemerov's indignation is not icy enough
to warrant comparison with Swift; it is rather Voltaire's
comic grimace with a strong dash of strictly American guf-
faw.

The element of wit, though hardly in so heavy a dos-
age as here, is a permanent element in Nemerov's poetry.
When it is so wholeheartedly indulged, it has a kind of fren-
zied purity. This example of reductio ad absurdum comes
off from sheer (and painstakingly achieved, for all that, one
imagines) gusto. Sometimes his verbal wit rattles tinnily in
serious lyrics, especially in some of the early work. But
in New and Selected Poems, consisting mostly of poems written or published within the last five years, he has managed
a tighter control, and the results--"if you want results"--
are thematically rich and prosodically strong.

Certainly the satirical gusto develops into something
rich and strange in "Suburban Prophecy":

> On Saturday, the power-mowers' whine
> Begins the morning. Over this neighborhood
> Rises the keening, petulant voice, begin
> Green oily teeth to chatter and munch the cud.
>
> Monsters, crawling the carpets of the world,
> Still send from underground against your blades
> The roots of things battalions green and curled
> And tender, that will match your blades with blades
> Till the revolted throats shall strangle on
> The tickle of their dead, till straws shall break
> Crankshafts like camels, and the sun go down
> On dinosaurs in swamps. A night attack
> Follows, and by the time the Sabbath dawns
> All armored beasts are eaten by their lawns.

War, city, nature--the familiar concerns this time presented
as sardonic prophecy. There are so many false-prophets
hawking their stuff in the Great American Wilderness these
days that the voice of God is hard to distinguish. Nemerov,
gifted with patience and good humor and a mature awareness
of his powers, is certainly succeeding in persuading, fooling,
or compelling some genuine voice into speech in his poems.
Whether that voice is in any sense divine may safely be left
to his readers to decide.

4. An Interview with Howard Nemerov

by Donna Gerstenberger

Originally published in Trace, January 1960.
Reprinted by permission of the author and of
Trace. Copyright (c) Villiers Publications, Ltd.
1960.

The value of an interview lies in the opinions expressed by a man who takes the practice of letters as an important matter: therefore, without benefit of scene, I offer
this recent interview with Mr. Nemerov.

Q. Is modern poetry obscure?

A. Some of it, no doubt, is difficult, more difficult than
    but a few examples from the past; and some of these dif-
    ficulties are rather arbitrary.   But I have got tired of
    hearing this question brought up as a charge against po-
    etry, because I have the distinct impression that the
    people who bring it up do not spend their leisure hours
    with Chaucer and Milton, but with the Reader's Digest
    and other comic books.   It's very much a comic-book
    question, maybe.

        I don't think, myself, that the excellence of poetry
    is measurable by the degree of its difficulty; on the oth-
    er hand, I enjoy hard poetry a good deal, and am not
    sympathetic to the commandments of the Simple school,
    which have so pronounced a way of beginning with Thou
    Shalt Not.   The poet must be allowed to choose any
    means he thinks he needs, if only because no one has

any way of stopping him.

Q. Is it worthwhile, then, for a magazine that is not a little magazine devoted to poetry to continue to publish poetry?

A. I think it is, but it depends what sort of result would satisfy the editors' expectations of the stuff. If a poem now and again gives pleasure to one or two or a hundred readers, then the publication of it seems worthwhile. If you think about the intimate nature of your own response to poems, you will see that the question of a 'mass audience' is merely statistical, and thus merely irrelevant, and thus merely absurd. People read poetry--if they do --one at a time.

Q. Where do you believe the audience for modern poetry is to be found?

A. I imagine that very few people read it, who don't try to write it. And I know from experience that people exist who try to write it but don't read any. That narrows things down pretty severely. I guess. But poetry, modern poetry, is fashionable right now in colleges and universities; students seem to care for it a great deal, as far as I'm able to tell.

Q. Do you really think, then, that the university helps create an audience for poetry?

A. It lets people know that poetry exists, doesn't it? On some campuses, in some English Departments, we seem to have established a kind of rabbinate for the sole purpose of interpreting The Waste Land; and the students do read the poem. Some of them probably enjoy poetry and go on with it after they leave school.

Q. Does the university do anything toward creating a potential poet, or does education stifle the creative impulse?

A.   This is another of those questions from the comic books.
     How can you tell?   Life is complicated enough, at least,
     that there are no easy answers to the questions why
     someone fails at something.   No doubt a university can
     powerfully ruin a poet just as it can a neuro-surgeon;
     but surely it's not the only place in which one can get
     ruined.

          But let's try a couple of general notions.   First,
     that poetry is an art.   It has a tradition, examples of
     it already exist; it is not something a young man or wom-
     an simply invents one morning.   In order to practice
     this art, you have to know what specimens of it look
     like, and some of this is taught in universities, along
     with a good deal of other stuff which the young poet may
     or may not need (something he can't find out, very of-
     ten, until later--until too late? who knows?).   Second,
     that if you look at the past you find that poets are al-
     most without exception very widely read.   They may or
     may not be educated men, but they furiously pursue
     whatever is in books, though their digestion of it does
     not resemble a scholar's.   Poets who did not have much
     formal education tend to read their Shakespeare hardest
     --Keats, for instance.   Probably the poet training in the
     university is conducting a kind of guerilla warfare--
     reading all the time, but not usually the stuff assigned
     to him to read.   What is a university, anyhow, but a lot
     of people in a library?

Q.   The university has often been identified and condemned
     as the support of many modern poets.   As a poet who
     is also a college teacher, would you care to comment
     on this?

A.   I like teaching, partly because it is--if you like it; and if you don't you won't be able to stand it, so the question won't come up--a fairly agreeable way of making a dollar, partly because it makes possible a more or less quiet life (if you have sense enough to stop talking after hours), and partly because teaching has been for me an education (Lord knows what it has been for my students). I never went to graduate school (he confessed, shyly, rolling his eyeballs a trifle).

As to condemning the college or university for keeping tame poets--for I suppose that to be the accusation--we have heard a great deal about that during the past several years.   There is a strong tendency among publishers, I have found, to think of poets as better off starving in garrets; it makes them (the publishers, that is) feel more real.   But until some foundation subsidises an air-conditioned garret, I guess some of us will have to make do with universities and colleges.   Probably many poets have been destroyed by teaching; certainly many more regard themselves as having been destroyed by teaching, but about that it is impossible to tell, since so many other factors--talent, for instance--enter in. And think how many poets must have been destroyed by, for example, the steel industry, advertising, social work, drink, or religion.   There seem to be no guarantees.

Q. Would you like to venture to name the best contemporary American poet?

A. For me to do so would be not only immodest, but very possibly inaccurate as well.

Q. Do you think there are problems peculiar to the American poet?

A. Never having been any other kind of poet, I cannot say, but I imagine it can never have been easy to be a poet,

anywhere or ever. One problem, possibly is trying
to sort out the good from the bad in contemporary work.
I know the cry is, as always, that it is hard for a poet
to get published, but all the same there seems to be an
awful lot of the stuff around, and the mere quantity may
tend to obscure how very good some of it is.

Q. Then you think that the notion that there is insufficient
outlet for the work of young poets is inaccurate?

A. Sufficient . . . insufficient? Take an arbitrary figure,
multiply it by the number of typewriters in the nation,
divide by the number of complaints . . . and so on. I
don't think I am a young poet any more (except by one
definition which says you are a young poet until you have
either a full professorship or grandchildren, whichever
comes first), so I may simply not be aware of the diffi-
culties people are facing; but despite a good deal of popular mythology I don't believe the woods are full of first-
rate manuscripts. Nor second-rate, for that matter.

Q. What is your opinion of the most assertive 'movement'
we have, the 'San Francisco' poets?

A. 'San Francisco' poetry is not subversive enough. Good
poetry always has a strong element of the subversive in
it--forces that make for a poetry which is anarchic and
archaic--forces that belong to childhood. There's not
enough dialectic in the work of the San Francisco group,
but I'm sure those poets have some talent.

Q. Do you think the popularity of jazz poetry helps or ob-
scures the cause of contemporary poetry?

A. I haven't heard too much of it, but I would say, by and
large, that jazz poetry is an amiable kind of foolishness.
It is all right to do these things if people get pleasure
from them, although I have no doubt that the music ob-

scures much of the poetry and that much of it deserves
to be.

Q.   I take it you don't feel the American poet suffers from
the absence of clearly defined 'movements' in poetry?

A.   I don't have much interest in 'movements.' People may
feel encouraged by belonging to something of the sort,
but if they have anything at all they must finish by de-
fining themselves against the movement. Maybe they
have to develop an orthodoxy before they can find out
what heresy attracts them most. Whatever other talents
poets may need, a talent for sitting in a room alone is
very frequently one they have.

Part II:

BOOK REVIEWS OF WORKS BY HOWARD NEMEROV

1.   The Image and the Law

a)   Reviewed by F. C. Golffing

Mr. Nemerov tells us--on the dust-jacket, of all places--that he dichotomizes the "poetry of the eye" and the "poetry of the mind," and that he attempts to exhibit in his verse the "ever-present dispute between two ways of looking at the world." Though usually skeptical of programmatic statements, I find this particular one quite serviceable as a clue--a "way in"--to the plexus of Nemerov's poetry.

The dichotomy itself is fashionable, and it is peculiar. It has almost assumed the status of doctrine in the work of Wallace Stevens, who disassociates mind and eye while paying homage to both and in the work of W. C. Williams, who, while exploiting sensory perception, makes short work of the mind. There are other poets--none of them of comparable rank--who would, on the basis of the same antinomy, dismiss sense-perception for the sake of pure intellection.

What matters here is not the individual emphasis of the poet but the fact that the underlying assumption is unsound. Eye and mind are not two contrary ways of looking at the world but two interdependent modes of prehension, the

perceptual mode subserving the conceptual and normative.
The poet who tears the two modes asunder and presents them
as inimical commits a meaningless act of violence, which is
likely to vitiate the intellectual framework of his poetry.

The fact that both Stevens and Williams have written
a great deal of excellent verse cannot be regarded as proof
of the soundness of their methods: verse as good as theirs
or better has been written on principles that are not generally recognized as either flimsy or perverse (vide Shelley,
Swinburne, Whitman, Hart Crane). While there is evidently
no simple correlation between a writer's doctrine and his poetic practice, it is equally plain that a half-baked or wrong-
headed philosophy will tend to have an ill effect on his manner of composition. I am convinced that most of the failures
in the work of both Stevens and Williams must be traced to
a defect, not in sensibility or formal mastery, but in envis-
agement or, as Kenneth Burke might say, poetic strategy.

Being largely under the sway of Wallace Stevens, Mr.
Nemerov has appropriated not only the basic dichotomy of
that poet but also his special tactics of treating ideas and
perceptions severally and oppositionally. About half of his
pieces deal with "images," while the other half are concerned with the "law," i. e. , the normative function of the
mind. I can discern no methodological connection between
the two sets, not even the dialectical one of active contrasts
moving toward some kind of synthesis. Not a few of the
"images"--that is, the strictly descriptive or anecdotal
pieces--are quite good in their whimsical way; though rarely
witty they have to their credit a certain mordancy, acumen,
and lightness of touch. Stylistically they hover between Stevens and K. Rexroth, with occasional sallies--no spoils re-
sulting--into Empson's domain. When Mr. Nemerov deals

with ideas he is as a rule less satisfactory; partly through
simple lack of style--his identification with Rexroth becomes
intolerable at times, especially in his most ambitious attempt, "The Frozen City," which despite several impressive
lines is a towering monument to bathos, cf. "Moving, I saw /
The murderer staring at his knife, / Unable to understand,
and a banker / Regarding a dollar bill with fixed / Incompre-
hension," etc. --partly through conceptual confusion, as in
"The Place of Value," where a plea for relevance is made
in the most irrelevant terms: the neurotic individual versus
the healthy statistician, fortuitous versus expiatory death,
etc. Yet, oddly enough, it is in this category that we must
look for Nemerov's best poems: "Warning: Children at
Play," "An Old Photograph" and, particularly, "Lot's Wife"
--poems which suggest that ideation may after all be this poet's forte and that, by turning division of mind and eye into
collaboration, he may yet achieve a fine body of poetry.
"Lot's Wife" deserves to be quoted in full; though ostensibly
an animadversion on religious and other revivals, the piece
rises far above the level of controversy and assumes the
grave beauty characterizing all consummate symbolic statements:

> I have become a gate
> To the ruined city, dry,
> Indestructible by fire.
> A pillar of salt, a white
> Salt boundary stone
> On the edge of destruction.
>
> A hard lesson to learn,
> A swift punishment; and many
> Now seek to escape
> But look back, or to escape
> By looking back: and they
> Too become monuments.

Remember me, Lot's wife,
Standing at the furthest
Commark of lust's county.
Unwilling to enjoy,
Unable to escape, I make
Salt the rain of the world.

b)   Reviewed by William Arrowsmith

The duality of image and law, "the way of the eye
and that of the mind," is, for Mr. Nemerov, finally recon-
·cilable in poetry.   The last poem of his book belatedly but
directly deals with the title and is an index of what he is up
to:

There is the world, the dream, and the one law.
The wish, the wisdom, and things as they are.

Inside the cave the burning sunlight showed
A shade and forms between the light and shade,

Neither real nor false nor subject to belief:
If unfleshed, boneless also, not for life

Or death or clear idea.   But as in life
Reflexive, multiple, with the brilliance of

The shining surface, an orchestral flare.
It is not to believe, the love or fear

Or their profoundest definition, death;
But fully as orchestra to accept,

Making an answer, even if lament,
In measured dance, with the whole instrument.

Syntactically and verbally the poem is Stevens'; the Platonism is anybody's; there can be no quarrel with derivation as explicit as this.   The poem is not difficult, the language is hard at work, the perception is steady and developed and yet, except as a good gloss upon the image and the law, the poem does not come off.   I cannot help but think that the blame lies in Nemerov's failure to provide this poem and others with significant integrity by making his myth his own: whose image, whose law?   His poles, like Stevens' guitar, have a way of becoming blueprints rather than agents of perfecting insight.   And as such, they are more nearly akin to the law than to the image.

A large number of his poems are, in this way, imperfect: correct, self-contained, but without substantial conviction, the derivations become too extensive, too good copies: Auden and Stevens are too persistently present for judgment or comfort.   Among his lighter poems, nice irony and effective diction control both "History of a Literary Movement" and "Metropolitan Sunday; A Chromium-Plated-Hat" is pure clinker and banality.   Similarly, the book as a whole is spotty and poorly-proportioned, the talent still promiscuous and unattached.   This is all the more regrettable since five or six poems, particularly "Europe" and "The Frozen City," have a genuine distinction and formal balance. This is good, for both poems are ambitious and also, I believe, both recent, in evidence of a bias decided upon and taken.   He has both unmistakable talent and promise.   Nor do I mean this disarmingly.

2.   The Melodramatists

a)   Reviewed by Isa Kapp

> This review originally appeared as "A Lively Ir-
> reverance" in Commentary, June 1949.   It is re-
> printed by permission of Commentary.   Copyright
> (c) 1949 by the American Jewish Committee.

At a time when the most trivial occasions seem to
call forth cataclysmic pronouncements on our atrophied values, perished glories, and unusable traditions, Howard Nemerov takes the position that, in the midst of the fragmentary
and the dissonant, it is possible to preserve one's identity
and make a productive start.   In the crisis of The Melodramatists, when the pillars and the rebels of society come
face to face, he turns his own attention to a fugue for piano
in which the polyphonic voices show "an inexorable confidence in their not quite harmonious world."

Though Nemerov's satire on a Bostonian family makes
its (by now traditional) gesture of protest against the bour-
geois world, most of its esprit and virtuosity is directed
against the extreme avenues of flight and return resorted to
by the residents.   The Catholic Church, representing one
possible bulwark against Protestant materialism and common
sense, is described as being at its best subtle and worldly,
at its worst furtive, and in any case helpless to solve human
problems, even in its own terms.   Its typical priest is seen
as a kind of floorwalker of religion, fussy, efficient, and

diplomatic, tempering with appropriate rhetoric the dogma of
exchange (one truth for another) and refund (absolution for
yielded sins).

The elder sister in The Melodramatists is betrayed
by her romantic hope in the spiritual discipline of the Roman
Church; the younger is defeated by its opposite, a love of
empiricism and investigation for its own sake.   Susan's af-
fair with a refugee psychoanalyst is portentously treated as
a reenactment of the primal fall in Eden.   The analyst is
Satan, still tendering the original apple of sexual knowledge
whose fruit corrodes the spirit and complicates the heart.
A victim of professional self-hatred, Dr. Einman believes
that it is his business to render the extraordinary mediocre,
to amputate "another limb of humanity" (a suspicion Mary
McCarthy once put much more vigorously: "Oh my God . . .
preserve me in disunity").   He is also amoral; through his
intimacy with pain and decay (he was a prisoner at Auschwitz and "not one feature seemed unblemished, untouched by
experience, there were no blanks in the face") he has been
shot onto a plane beyond morality, which is a luxury of the
surface life.   On the other hand, this very scientist, who
uses his patients more for research than for therapy, is the
reasonable advocate of Nemerov's theory of moderateness,
of self-possession in the face of paradox and aberration.
"Everything absolute," he points out, "belongs to death."
But this wisdom is lost on an existentialist Satan for whom
the opening up of infinite possibility ("anything can happen")
is synonymous with uprooting.   Nemerov, too, seems willing to place a tragic weight on the loss of innocence, and to
assume that knowledge either corrupts or is futile.

Futility is the real target of this satire, and that is
why the book, despite the tense formal perfection that ad-

mirably exploits at all points the logic of the absurd, often
appears to be charging at windmills. There is among all
these romantic tragedians not enough smugness, vice, or re-
spectability to make a battle worth while. The "emperor,"
in this case, is willing to testify to his own nakedness, and
the "new clothes" are the sheerest hypothetical fabric of the
novelist. Nevertheless, simply by going through the motions
of masking and unmasking, Nemerov turns up haphazard
sleazy undergarments in unexpected places.

His most Huxleyan thrust is against the Protestant
patriarch who escapes from the contradictions of his break-
fast table autocracy to a Nirvana of hot baths and insanity.
In that retreat, ironic fate finally catches up with him, and
the old violator of his family's privacy is forbidden to lock
even his bathroom door against doctors and attendants.
Nemerov throughout his novel makes the point that it is in-
creasingly impossible to achieve privacy in modern society.
Thus, by a sleight of hand, he scoops the blackmailing but-
ler out of detective stories into his true place as a challenge
to the privacy of his employer: the obscene intruder who
makes up the beds. And in the end, no privacy remains,
even for sin or death.

The melodramatists converge like puppets toward the
farce of the climax. A tranquil old whore pulls the strings,
bumps together the heads of science and religion, and exe-
cutes a coup d'état in what was once a proper Bostonian
home, and later a house of correction. Of course this is
too shrewd, too inversely logical for an authentic novel, but
it serves as a springboard for Nemerov's dialectics. Something can be said for the role of the minor novelist as critic
rather than as generator. Though The Melodramatists is
stiff and unrelaxed (it has no ebb and flow, no solid prosaic

stretches of narrative) and well-guarded (it will never be
caught in a simple sentence or direct commitment), it flour-
ishes a lively irreverence in the face of our contemporary
pieties.

b)   Reviewed by Harrison Smith

Originally published as "Two Fall From Grace,"
Saturday Review, April 2, 1949. Reprinted by
permission of Saturday Review. Copyright (c)
1949, The Saturday Review Associates, Inc.

It is with some trepidation that the conscientious reviewer opens the first novel of a young American who has
won some recognition for his poetry and for short stories
and essays that could not have been published in any of the
mass-circulation magazines. As an editor of the magazine
Furioso, he might be considered one of the leaders of that
group of youthful writers whose doleful and angry approach
to the American scene and whose obsession with despair have
been attacked by several critics, including the writer of this
review. On the jacket of his book Mr. Nemerov asserts
that he is "dignified, commonplace, and thoroughly middle-
class," but there is certainly nothing commonplace either in
his manner of thought or in his talents as an entertaining
and somewhat satanic satirist of American life and morals.

The Melodramatists is, in fact, the kind of novel we
have been hoping for a long time would finally emerge from
one of our new writers. It is inevitable that it will be compared with some of the work of Evelyn Waugh and Aldous
Huxley, though Mr. Nemerov is by implication more serious

than the first writer and less abstruse than the second, at least as Mr. Huxley is revealed in his later books.   It should be stated at the outset that The Melodramatists is an unblushingly shocking novel, though none of its more carnal scenes are visualized, and it might well be considered profane by those who think that religion or the science of psychiatry are not proper subjects for high comedy.

The story, apart from its grotesque and delicate embroideries, can be easily summarized.   It has to do with the fall from grace by separate paths of the two daughters of Nicholas Boyne when that head of a large and opulent Boston mansion was sent away with the girls' mother to an institution for the elderly insane.   In the first chapter Nicholas's son vanishes by joining the Canadian Army, and does not return until the end, when he finds his dignified home turned momentarily into a brothel and his adulterous wife in the arms of his best friend.

This leaves Susan and Claire to pursue their separate paths, unhindered by advice or chaperonage.   Susan, sleek and beautiful, had the self-sufficiency of a tame cat.   With ease and rapidity she was seduced by her amorous and elderly psychiatrist.   Dr. Einman was a charlatan, to be sure, but there is enough resemblance between his lush verbal use of the more abstrusely morbid sins of the flesh and the conversational byplay of a few living psychiatrists in their unguarded moments, to give this repulsive and loveless man a sort of pathetic reality.

Her more saintly and perhaps frigid sister, Claire, contemplates Susan's downfall with horror, and the sight of the doctor leaving her sister's bedroom after midnight leaves her in an emotional state that induces her to find a more intellectual ecstasy in prayer.   Since she is attracted to the

Catholic faith by the conceptions of divine love, sin, and redemption, she accepts a scholarly priest as her tutor.   The
Bishop himself finally takes notice of this lonely and wealthy
convert and uses the almost empty house to the advantage of
Christian charity.   The charity that is unhappily selected,
the correction and salvation of "fallen women," leads to the
satirically tragic ending, which is as absurd and as naughty,
since the reader has been absorbing discourses and argu-
ments on virtue and piety, as can be imagined.

The Melodramatists is true satire, written in the spirit of comedy, and it deals with sacred and profane love in
terms that are not unfamiliar to the readers of many modern
novels.   Mr. Nemerov perhaps discourses sometimes at too
great length on his store of knowledge of almost everything
from music to religious literature and black magic.   But his
display of verbal fireworks, or mental gymnastics, if you
please, cannot disguise the essential humanity and brilliance
of this book.

3. Guide to the Ruins

a) Reviewed by Vivienne Koch

Howard Nemerov's new collection, Guide to the Ruins, points its direction in the title. Like Mr. Hayes, Mr. Moore, Mr. Schwartz, and some others he is deeply disturbed by the character of contemporary experience.[1] War is a looming antagonist and image in his work. Like Hayes, too, he is interested in Jewish themes, or rather, in assessing what it means to be Jewish now. But there is no self-pity in his bitter appraisals, and he is good at epigrammatic thrusts on a variety of social evils. A particularly sharp one, somewhat in the style of Hardy's late anti-war epigrams, is "Peace in Our Time." "On a Text: Jonah IV, xi" is elegantly savage in its understated attack on Philistines.

But the epigram does not exhaust Mr. Nemerov's ambitions. He is diligent, and explores with considerable ingenuity the possibilities of a great many traditional forms-- sonnets, elegies, and fable being among them. In terms of the remarkable advances represented by Guide to the Ruins over his somewhat academic first collection, The Image and

The Law, I should guess that Mr. Nemerov will eventually
prove a worthy contender for high honors among the poets of
his generation.   While I do not think we can expect any en-
largement of the capacity for sensuous apprehension--that
first gift to the poet which is given and not earned--his sincerity and his sharp intellectual control will, no doubt, reap
their proper increments.

In this collection he has not yet entirely mastered his
influences, especially the Yeats of the Crazy Jane poems
(see the able "The Second Best Bed" for this) or the Pound
of "Mauberly" compounded with the Eliot of the Prufrock
poems.   Sometimes, however, as in the tender "Carol," he
writes a poem that is traditional in its lyric structure but
entirely original for the way the language is disposed to a
keenly-sighted aesthetic end.   The closing cinquain of the ten
which compose the poem will demonstrate his quality:

> For there was born at Bethlehem
> Silence and night
> The world and heaven's single stem
> That to both kingdoms we might then
> Say Amen.

Note

1.   Miss Koch was referring to Nicholas Moore, Recollec-
     tions of the Gola (London: Editions Poetry, 1951);
     Alfred Hayes, Welcome to the Castle (New York:
     Harper, 1951); and Delmore Schwartz, Vaudeville for
     a Prince (New York: New Directions, 1951).

b)   Reviewed by I. L. Salomon

Howard Nemerov suffers from poetic schizophrenia.
He wouldn't be caught dead with a lyre in his hand.   A university wit, he stifles his considerable gifts by exploiting not
the excellences but the defects his masters (Eliot, Auden,
Tate) have imposed on a generation of poets.   Guide to the
Ruins contains only a handful of first-rate poems; too many
others lack the discipline of the writer's art.   Good pieces
are marred by a slovenly intrusion of slang and awkward
phrase, and fail, since Mr. Nemerov's superb ear dares not
be true to an authentic impulse.   He slights accent and
rhythm for the sake of being fashionable.

That Mr. Nemerov has an instinct for perfection is
quite apparent in his war lyrics.   These are organically sustained.   What man has made corruptible in this little life is
told with mordant wit and savage satire.   In "The Bacterial
War," "A Fable of the War," "The Hero Comes Home in
His Hamper, and Is Exhibited at the World's Fair" his anger
is controlled; his eye, objective; his spirit, fierce.   Intense
excitement went into the making of these poems, as in "Still
Life" and in the psychological double-feature "Trial and
Death."

But Mr. Nemerov suffers from a dichotomy in personality.   He must be modern and his modernity consists also
of a studied carelessness in expression.   In different poems
where the fusion of language and image is precise, such slang,

bad syntax, and doggerel obtain:

   (1) Up from Egypt then did come
       All the chosen and then some

   (2) They . . . (cockroaches) . . . can
       be drowned but not
       Without you hold them under
       quite some time

   (3) When my teeth began to grow
       That first opinion had to go

It is incredible that a skilful poet would knowingly obtrude such haphazard writing on the public. In the name of modernity, it is done by design. Had Mr. Nemerov rewritten his poorly-made poems Guide to the Ruins would have been an excellent book.

4. Federigo, or the Power of Love

Reviewed by Herbert F. West

A modern comedy . . . this novel originates from the
tangled webs mortals weave when first they practice to de-
ceive. Its rather flippant moral, if it may be said to have
one, is that all women are alike in the dark.

Julian and Sylvia Ghent, the protagonists, are two
people who live the glittering, unreal life of the modern New
York apartment dweller. The author depicts well the shadow
world of cocktail parties, Afghan hounds, pallid adulteries
carried on gravely and without conviction. This is the neighborhood where the psychoanalyst lives next door--ready, at
the drop of a large piece of currency, to listen to one's
self-pity.

Julian Ghent is an advertising man who is constantly
and somewhat sardonically amused and surprised at the absurdities in his sacred profession. "It's amazing what things
can go on in the human head, what battles and betrayals, all
in utter, lonely security." Sylvia, his childless wife, is a
young bored, woman with a past, and with nothing to do save
to fancy that she is quite, quite unhappy.

The novel, along with most contemporary fiction, is

78

about sex: "the great secret that everyone know, the Whore
of Babylon, the pleasure of Judas, the object of all movies,
the space between the lines of newspapers and the silences
of mother and father." At times it sounded almost as if
sex were being discovered for the first time.

Unhappy in marriage? Then should one take a mistress? Kill one's self? Take a world cruise? Live elsewhere under a new name? Redeem one's self by missionary
work in a malarial swamp? These are the alternatives Federigo presents to the hero.

And who is Federigo? A second self? Mephistopho-
les in modern dress? A Döppelgänger? Or a somewhat
pretentious literary device which covers a multitude of sins?

One begins by taking the story seriously, but soon the
reader perceives that Mr. Nemerov is spoofing the comedy
of modern life: psychoanalysis (the analyst, Dr. Mirabeau,
is a completely egotistical and irritating fool), modern marriage, private detectives, urban living, modern advertising
and other absurdities of our times. He certainly succeeds
at times in giving a brilliant if superficial and glossy picture of what goes on in the vacant minds of a certain New
York social set, which has nothing to do but to seek a titil-
lating kind of sexual excitement (generally unfulfilled), who
are bored, who get drunk, and who have innocent infantile
fantasies about love.

Mr. Nemerov is skillful in his portrayal of the Ham-
lets who write advertising copy, of the women whose modern
handbook is Freud on the one hand and Vogue on the other.
Federigo, or, The Power of Love, becomes at times, in a
Waughish sort of way, a rather hilarious pastiche with serious undertones.

5. The Salt Garden

a) Reviewed by Robert Hillyer

The third of Howard Nemerov's books of verse, The
Salt Garden is also his best. The general mood is dark,
sometimes as forbidding as a frozen plain that thaws, but
does not bloom, under occasional sunlight. It has the bleak
spaciousness of crags and sea--especially sea, which draws
out the poet's melancholy beyond himself and gives it the
feeling of common, rather than private, tragedy.

Mr. Nemerov's usual method might mislead the casual reader into terming it a "metaphysical" style, wherein,
as Dr. Johnson observed, "the most heterogeneous ideas are
yoked by violence together." The ideas that might seem
heterogeneous at first are drawn together by affinities and
associations shared by them all. For example, in "I Only
Am Escaped Alone to Tell Thee" (a quotation echoing Moby
Dick) we see at first in a dimly lighted hall the figure of a
woman of the mid-nineteenth century, stiff in the confines of
her whalebone corset. The theme of the sea is introduced
by the flawed mirror like "troubled water." Then the line,
"It was no rig for dallying" not only indicates the whalebone
of conventional restraint but also serves as a transition to

the whaleship, the slaughter of the whale and the sea. The
last four lines bring all the elements together: "the black
flukes of agony" of the dying whale are death struggles of
betrayed nature beating the air "till the light goes out."

I cite this poem not because it is the best but because
it extravagantly displays the device that the poet uses more
adroitly and simply elsewhere, for example in the title poem,
in "Dandelions," in the unforgettable "Midsummer's Day,"
throughout Part Two, and in the delicate ottava rima stanzas
of "The Gull."

The effective dialogue, "A Deposition," in Part Four,
is reminiscent of the philosophy of Anatole France's Revolt
of the Angels and Lord Acton's oft-quoted remark on absolute power. The last section, Part Five, relaxes into a
mood of retrospective tenderness in which "Central Park"
is especially moving.

The Salt Garden is an important and beautiful book.
Several of these poems seem to me destined for a long future.

b) Reviewed by Randall Jarrell

Originally published as "Recent Poetry." Yale
Review, Autumn 1955. Copyright 1955 by Mrs.
Randall Jarrell.

The Salt Garden, Howard Nemerov's third book of
poems, is very much the best of the three. The earlier
books were the products of intelligence and talent, but they
were tight, dry, and uneasy--you were always conscious of
omissions, abstentions, aversions, of the poet's looking for

some way to write and some subject to write about, and ending, always, with something people could call ironic.   (Whenever people use such words as dialectical, metaphysical,
dry, conceit, ironic about a new poem of Mr. Nemerov's,
he can tell that he has gone back to his old ways.) As you
read The Salt Garden you are impressed with how much the
poet has learned, how well he has developed: you can see
where he found out how to do some of the things he does--
he isn't, as yet, a very individual poet--and you can see
that they were the right places for him.   Behind the old poems there was a poet trying to write poetry; behind these
new ones there is a man with interests and experiences of
his own--that is, a poet who has learned to write poetry.
In his best poems his language and rhythms have a natural,
normal vigor, a quality that makes you think, "Yes, a lot of
good English poetry feels like this." When he is speaking of
the "deep woods" of this New World of ours, without hermits,
hunting kings, the woodcutter's or the witch's house--before
history, really--he says that here in the forest the mind

>   uneasily rests, as if a beast,
> Being hunted down, made tiredness and terror
> Its camouflage and fell asleep, and dreamed,
> At the terrible, smooth pace of the running dogs,
> A dream of being lost, covered with leaves,
> And hidden in a death like any sleep . . .

He looks at the "unlegended land" whose "common splendors
are comparable only to/ Themselves," and then moves on
through history and legend, deciding, always, that that too
hasn't happened here--that if we want it to happen we our-
selves will have to make it happen--and finishes,

>   Most probably
> Nothing will happen. Even the Fall of Man
> Is waiting, here, for someone to grow apples;

> And the snake, speckled as sunlight on the rock
> In the deep woods, still sleeps with a whole head
> And has not begun to grow a manly smile.

These last three lines are what the fairy tale calls a wonderful wonder, a marvelous marvel; I keep saying them over for
the way they sound and move. The snake is alive, and the
past is latent in him. (And now I want to say, as much in
surprise as in complaint: How did phrases like "the Fourth,
or Disney, Dimension"--or for that matter, like the Frost-
ish "this / Place is too old for history to know / Beans a-
bout"--get into a poem like this?)

I'd like to quote an ingenious and moving poem named
"And I Only Am Escaped Alone to Tell Thee," or some beau-
tiful or thoughtful parts of "The Quarry" or "The Pond" or
"Truth," but perhaps I had better let a short poem, "The
Cuckoo King," stand for all of them:

> My head made wilderness, crowned of weed
> And marigold, the world my witching bride
> And the half of my kingdom lying in the seed,
> I reap the great root of a planted pride.
>
> All earth broken under the harrow's heel,
> I through my comely kingdom went a-riding
> Out where the bearded grass climbed to rebel
> And the tall stalking flower fired from hiding.
>
> The world, O my daughter in the crooked nest,
> Bridles with lust, that you by force betray
> Me, weed and marigold, to the naked crest
> Where castles fall; but I will make this hay
> In husbandry beneath the rebel's height,
> Though all the hairs of my head stand upright.

That "world, O my daughter in the crooked nest" is pure
Thomas (almost the only Thomas in the book) but, like the
future, it works. The poem has a kind of emblematic force,
as if it were a King of Spades painted for "The White God-

dess." And now I must talk about the specter which is
haunting this particular book: middle and late Yeats; you
find half of Yeats' pet words and rhythms, his rhetorical use
of the word maybe, even. And whenever Mr. Nemerov sees
a gull he starts to sound like "The Wild Swans at Coole":
"Sweet are their bitter cries, / As their fierce eyes are
sweet; in their mere greed / Is grace, as they fall splendid-
ly to feed. / And sometimes I have seen them as they glide /
Mysterious upon a morning sea . . . ." This last is a
reminiscence of Yeats' "But now they drift on the still water
/ Mysterious, beautiful," of course, but doesn't it also
echo Bridges' lines about the frigates he saw from the summer house on the mound, as they glided murderously over
a calm sea? (I'm far from books, and go by memory
alone.) And the poet says, about another gull, that he had
"thought that image of the wild / Wave where it beats the
air / Had come, brutal, mysterious"; the poem in which
these lines occur, "The Salt Garden," is what a composer
would call "Yeatsiana."

And is this so bad? No--Yeats has spoiled some of
the poems, but has helped the poetry. It's odd that the poet
should need or wish or consent to this much help this late;
perhaps it is because he is a late-blooming, youthful-seem-
ing poet from whom one can expect, soon, poems even better
than the best two or three in this book.

6. Mirrors and Windows

a) Reviewed by Reed Whittemore

When Howard Nemerov was younger it was not evident to his readers or perhaps to Nemerov himself that he
would turn into a nature poet. The visible models, from
Wordsworth to Frost, seemed as foreign to his intellectual
and verbal manners as they would well seem. Indeed it was
as a smart (and his elders thought too smart) rebel against
the clean outdoor simplicities or the charting of emanations
from bushes that he got into verse at all; and his early spirit of unbushiness did not distinguish him much from his contemporaries at Harvard, which he attended, or Yale, which
he frequented.

Then came what looked like a change of heart, a
change evident in his last volume, The Salt Garden. The
change was indicated by a new interest in the difficult but
relatively straightforward art of description. Against his apparent earlier inclinations he deliberately cultivated the naturalist's as distinguished from the metaphysicist's eye; and
if visited in Vermont he could be found out on long walks
naming things. Before the switch he could, to be sure, have
been found out on the same walks, but not for the same rea-

son: instead of naming and characterizing the birds about
him he would endow them with the trappings of paradox and
analogy.   After the switch he continued to be interested in
paradox and analogy, but he was more grateful for the birds
he started with than he had been.

Of natural analogies the new volume is full.   Nature
is, as I think Milton Babbitt pointed out, frequently merely
a projection of self; the poet finds what he wants to find in
nature, and what he wants to find is more than apt to be
what he is or would like to be.   If he is a romantic he is
probably not conscious of the analogues he is drawing (it sat-
isfies my ego to think of all romantics as unconscious).   If
he is a Nemerov he is hyperconscious of them.   But in either event he does establish a relationship; the outer and the
inner landscapes tend to merge, to make an order in which
a common body of law and truth prevails.   All the medieval
analogues did this openly and rigorously; their modern coun-
terparts are mostly sneaky and haphazard.   But in the old
and the new alike human nature seeks out its extra-human
natural models or equivalents.

What does Mr. Nemerov find in nature with which he
may personally be compared?--birds, mountains, isolated
trees, statues and more birds.   Birds especially.   And what
is the relationship of these mostly birds to their environ-
ment?   They are the ones who are out of it all, working out
their lone destinies without reference to or even despite their
surroundings.   The surroundings are bare beach, bare rock,
bare sky; or if they are not simply barren they are demo-
cratic, low, dirty, menacing, humdrum.   And what do the
mostly birds do in these surroundings? Well, the birds in the
town dump make the most of a bad situation:

> . . . But I will add
> That wild birds, drawn to the carrion
>   and flies.
> Assemble in some numbers here, their
>   wings
> Shining with light, their flight enviably
>   free.
> Their music marvelous, though sad,
>   though strange.

The tree in a world of change stands firm. The sandpipers
on the beach make a go of escaping the ravenous sea ("I
have never seen one caught"), and of feeding themselves as
they do so; this is their skill, and it is a great skill, the
source of their beauty:

> . . . When suddenly they turn
> In unison, all their bellies shine
> Like mirrors flashing white with signals
> I cannot read, but I wish them well.

As for mountains, they make a business of calmly "rising
above the storm / To the region of serenity and splendor."
In summary, these natural isolationists or independents prac-
tise their independence successfully and become, thus, models for their human equivalents, poets particularly.

Nemerov's various birds have a good deal in common
with Yeats's swans, Keats's nightingales and a horde of other by now thoroughly conventionalized independents; and because they do one may reasonably ask to what extent their
presence in Nemerov's work may be attributed to a view of
things that Nemerov personally, privately, in the regions of
his "natural" heart espouses. Are his poems of the heart
or the will? Fortunately Nemerov himself questions his
identifications, his sallyings forth into what he "is." When
he does so he takes to discussing his art and his validity;
he takes to worrying about whether he as a poet is alienated

from himself as himself, whoever he may be.   Thus a good
many poems turn on themselves.   They consider the poet
writing about what he is writing about, and so forth.

Several years ago, in a short, satiric, prose piece
about how to write a novel, Nemerov was similarly taken by
the problem of the creator's identity.   In this he describes
himself seated at his monstrous machine (a typewriter, and
also, if you will, a symbol of artifice) with his cigaret and
coffee, preparing to open up his heart.   All these appurte-
nances for the great unveiling loom larger than the unveiling
itself, and the longer he sits before the machine and smokes
the cigarets and drinks the coffee, the less clear does it
seem to him that there is anything to unveil except what the
machine and the cigaret and the coffee may themselves discover.   He appears, thus, at least to himself, as something
of an alien to his own authorial image.

These themes of alienation and identity are to our
time what love and the ravages of time were to Shakespeare's;
that is, they are subjects one writes poems about if one
writes poems; they are the matter with which one begins,
daily, over and over again, much as the housewife begins
with the cooking of eggs and bacon.   For there is nothing
that the modern poet has to confront more regularly than his
loneliness and displacement.   Accordingly these confronta-
tions soon come to have a ritualistic air about them.   The
poet goes out in the morning and looks for the occasion, the
object, the scene in which he may discover his predicament,
then pay homage to it.   Now in a less thoughtful poet than
Nemerov the homage would, and frequently does, take the
form of a lament.   In Nemerov on the other hand the rhetorical or lyric side of the business is of less consequence
than the metaphysical side.   The new book has two or three

poems in it that could be called chants, but they are neither
representative nor, I think especially distinguished.   The
best poems (with one or two exceptions) are more analytical
than lyrical.   This is not to say that they are not, or should
not be, poems, but that, as poems, they are dominantly in-
vestigations rather than assertions.   Sometimes, in fact,
their assertions are their weaknesses; the <u>declaration</u> that

>   . . . We sublimate--sublime!--all tidal
>   waves,
>   Tornadoes, tremblors of the earth, for
>   good
>   And all, finding the separateness that
>   saves
>   Garden and city from the wilderness
>   Where lust and wisdom tremble to un-
>   dress:--
>   So may we die before both Fall and
>   Flood

rings less true to my middle ear than the <u>observation</u> that

>   . . . each man
>   thought bitterly about primitive
>   simplicity
>   and decadence, and how he had been
>   ruined
>   by civilization and forced by circum-
>   stances
>   to drink and smoke and sit up all night
>   inspecting those perfectly arbitrary
>   cards
>   until he was broken-winded as a trout
>   on a rock
>   and had no use for the doctrines of
>   Jean Jacques
>   Rousseau, and could no longer afford
>   a savagery whether noble or not; some
>   would never batter that battered copy
>   of Walden
>   again.

In the former the poet is showing his hand, or at least saying that he is.   In the latter he is doing nothing of the kind,

and his detachment (if you will, his alienation) from "each
man" seems to me to be perfectly suited to his poetic psyche
or whatever. What the former passage lacks, to put it
bluntly, is irony, the essential ingredient of the alien's make-
up.

And yet irony is, by itself, easy--and the latter passage has a good deal more than irony. It is from "A Day
on the Big Branch," an instructive and persuasive example
of the later Nemerov being seriously ironic--detached from
and yet sympathetic to the object of irony, in this case a
group of ill-at-ease Rousseauists. In his earlier days Nemerov was frequently merely detached; the world was something to ridicule; his poetic ritual took the form of a (dignified) tongue lashing. Now he is mellower, humbler, wiser--
like one of Shakespeare's good dukes, though without a country to govern. This suggest to me, perhaps wrongly, that
he is, in his own fashion, working his way out of the alien-
ist's cave. I do not mean by this that his next volume will
be devoid of irony, alienation, and all that, but that his development seems to involve coming to terms with, living with,
even making a good thing of alienation rather than sitting
back and bemoaning it, as do most of his contemporaries.

Mirrors and Windows is not the work of a "younger
poet." Nemerov has thoroughly established himself in it as
a poet of the long poem, the poem that is not an assertion
of a simple lyric position but a dialogue, a leisurely confab-
ulation, a weekend excursion in verse to the mountains of
self. Such a poem may suffer--as all long poems are apt
to suffer--simply from being mature, considerate, etc.; and
I think it is not impossible that Nemerov is working up to
something terribly long and dull. But that time is not yet.
And if he can find in verse, as in his novels, narrative, dra-

matic excuses for even more extended meditations than the
present ones, then there would seem to be no limit to what
he can successfully pull off.   The verse comes easy to him.
The matter is there.   And he is apparently a very unhappy
man when he is not writing.

b)   Reviewed by Carolyn Kizer

Originally published as "Nemerov: the Middle of
the Journey," Poetry, December 1958.   Reprinted
by permission of the author and the editor of
Poetry.   Copyright 1958 by The Modern Poetry
Association.

With this book, his fourth, Howard Nemerov now belongs to that group of poets who are most difficult to review.
To express joy in the accomplished poems, yet receive them
ungraciously!   For, alas, the homage a serious reviewer
pays to a serious poet is a vigorous appraisal.   Still, the
poems must be handled with care, care in many of its meanings: mental effort, a sense of responsibility, solicitude,
affection, and concern.   Nemerov's own criticism has been
distinguished by these qualities, so there is the added obliga-
tion of trying to serve him as well as he has served other
poets.

Howard Nemerov is brave, intelligent, resourceful,
crafty, accomplished and grown-up.   He not only takes
chances with poems and ideas, he is unflinching: The poem,
"A Day on the Big Branch," provides us with, among other
things, a long, frank and tenderly ironic look at himself and
his contemporaries: the generation that was abruptly certi-
fied as adult in 1941, and that felt like surplus property from

1945 on. How many of us marked or saved this poem when
it appeared in <u>Poetry</u> because through it we saw our own unpoetic lives glowing with poetry? Hu Shih once said that to
arouse sentiment, the speaker must not be sentimental about
himself, or must have the art to conceal his feelings.

Though Nemerov uses technique and style to conceal
his feelings, occasionally he uses them to conceal the absence of feeling, when the motive seems to be a poem-for-
poem's sake. Then his equipment stands, polished but empty, like armor in the hall: the mechanical writing of "A
Primer of the Daily Round" (the kind of thing that most of
the younger English writers can toss off before tea); the long
poem, "Orphic Scenario," where no amount of forcing can
mobilize the dead-tired ideas; the rather limp self-consciousness of most of the Orient-influenced poems, as if they were
written on borrowed energy from an imperfectly assimilated
world. The long, discursive poem, "To Lu Chi," has a
grave and thoughtful central theme, muffled by too many un-
necessary lines. Certain phrases and tags are embarrassing:
"this somehow seems oddly Chinese . . ." "your words
have not failed / to move me with their justice and their
strength . . ." "so no / Goodbye, Lu Chi, and thank you
for your poem." Though Nemerov may clog the poem with
these bits of debris from time to time, there are lovely intervals when the flow is quite pellucid:

> And then you bring, by precept and example,
> Assurance that a reach of mastery,
> Some still, reed-hidden and reflective stream
> Where the heron fishes in his own image,
> Always exists. I have a sight of you,
> Your robes tucked in your belt, standing
> Fishing that stream, where it is always dawn
> With a mist beginning to be burned away
> By the lonely sun . . .

The hard fact remains that many of the long poems are too long. The shorter pieces show that he has a firm sense of dramatic structure, but in poems like "The Loon's Cry" or "Ahasuerus" the thrust of the poem is hampered by a good deal of off-side activity: whole stanzas of near-irrelevancy wander in, the focus shifts, the intensity diminishes. Sometimes because he does not trouble to whip a line, he sends a stanza to do a line's work. Sometimes when he is preoccupied with exposition, or with over-explicit ironies, the poetry flattens out into prose. Nemerov has what one might call an untrammeled intellect; he is capable of convincing himself that a sensibility or a concept is sufficiently poetic in itself: the poem becomes a vehicle to carry these responses or ideas. But when he subordinates his intellect to the verbal and linear demands of the poem, the result is a magnificently sustained, fulfilled poem like "Brainstorm":

> The house was talking, not to him he thought,
> But to the crows; the crows were talking back
> In their black voices. The secret might be out:
> Houses are only trees stretched on the rack
> And once the crows knew, all nature would know.
> Fur, leaf and feather would invade the form,
> Nail rust with rain and shingle warp with snow,
> Vine tear the wall, till any straw-borne storm
> Could rip both roof and rooftree off and show
> Naked to nature what they had kept warm . . .

That passage, with its felicitous echo of Hardy, is ripped from the center of a poem of thirty-nine lines. Most of Nemerov's long poems would be greatly strengthened if they were pared to more nearly this length.

Although Nemerov's ear is not always listening as hard as it should, his eye is, in Dr. Williams' phrase, infinitely penetrant:

> People are putting up storm windows now,
> Or were, this morning, until the heavy rain
> Drove them indoors. So, coming home at noon,
> I saw storm windows lying on the ground,
> Frame-full of rain; through the water and glass
> I saw the crushed grass, how it seemed to stream
> Away in lines like seaweed on the tide . . .

Or these lines, from "The Town Dump":

>   . . . From cardboard tenements,
> Windowed with cellophane, or simply tenting
> In paper bags, the angry mackerel eyes
> Glare at you out of stove-in, sunken heads
> Far from the sea; the lobster, also, lifts
> An empty claw in his most minatory
> Of gestures; oyster, crab and mussel shells
> Lie here in heaps, savage as money hurled
> Away at the gate of hell. If you want results,
> These are results . . .

That magnificent line about money! But, oh, the flatness of
those "results." This trick of word repetition in Nemerov
is nearly always a signal that his mind is playing fast and
loose with his poem: " . . . you may say / There should
be ratios. You may sum up / The results, if you want results. But I will add . . . " This passage of "fill" occurs
later in the poem, perhaps appropriately in a poem about a
dump. But, leafing through his book, one finds: "modern
American rocks, and hard as rocks . . . " "never batter
that battered copy of <u>Walden</u> again . . . " "a venomous
tense past tense," "Shadows emerge and merge . . . "
"Miraculous result would have resulted . . . " "Could happen only as they let it happen, / Refused to let it happen
. . . " and so on. Nemerov, now that he is mature,
should renounce the verbal playground. However, the kind
of mind which puns easily, can, under pressure, produce the
well-wrought irony and the stern paradox which turns the
whole world upside down:

On Sunday, the power-mowers' whine
Begins the morning. Over this neighborhood
Rises the keening, petulant voice, begin
Green oily teeth to chatter and munch the cud.

Monsters, crawling the carpets of the world,
Still send from underground against your blades
The roots of things battalions green and curled
And tender, that will match your blades with blades
Till the revolted throats shall strangle on
The trickle of their dead, till straws shall break
Crankshafts like camels, and the sun go down
On dinosaurs in swamps. A night attack
Follows, and by the time the Sabbath dawns
All armored beasts are eaten by their lawns.

This is the kind of writing that separates the men from the
boys: unusual syntax firmly manipulated, artful punctuation,
a texture clarified but never thin, an almost arrogant virtuosity. The poet, engaged in the sunlit nightmare of the contemporary world, both hotly observes it and coolly notes it
down. Certain poems of Wallace Stevens, Stanley Kunitz,
Richard Wilbur, come to mind . . . That marvelous quality,
opulent yet rigorous, of twentieth-century pentameter at its
best.

c) Reviewed by Norman Rosten

Originally published in Venture, III, Spring 1959.
Reprinted by permission of the author.

This new volume by Howard Nemerov is called Mirrors and Windows: mirrors to catch the sharp reflections
of one's face, windows to look out upon the wider landscape
of man in context with nature and history. Or, to those
probing for a further symbolism, we have a double glass:

one deflecting, reminding of the personal impasse, the other
allowing us to see through and freely beyond.   Close-up or
distant, the view here is enormously satisfying.

The real value of Nemerov's poetry, it seems to me,
is its reasonableness; the way John Donne strikes us as being reasonable: true feeling tempered by modesty, and a
directness of craft.

For much of modern poetry has been a battle of ex-
tremes.   We have had the over-simplified low voltage prac-
titioners with their rhyme and meter traditionally and weari-
ly correct; or the super-Dylan Thomas flailing of arms and
scrambling of metaphor school that has resulted in what I
would call the exhaustive method.

Nemerov is intelligent without being heavy-handed or
showy; he has wit; he employs a marvelously exact verbal
touch, with subtle rhythms, so that the weight of every line
hangs, like a Calder mobile, in true balance to the whole.
The impression is one of the author contentedly himself--a
confidence reflected on every page of a book that has variety
and range.

There is a sense of man and his generation struck
home with wry humor, nostalgia, and the fatalism of time,
in the narrative "A Day on the Big Branch," which opens:

> Still half drunk, after a night at cards,
> with the grey dawn taking us unaware
> among our guilty kings and queens, we drove
> far North in the morning, winners, losers,
> to a stream in the high hills, to climb up to a place
> one of us knew, with some vague view
> of cutting losses or consolidating gains
> by the old standard appeal to the wilderness . . .

This is verse handled with knowledge and ease, which knows
how to set a scene and carry an idea to the end.   It is a

call to memory, rugged and somehow endearing, that even
the non-drinkers will value.   Another fine narrative is a discourse on esthetics entitled "To Lu Chi."

In the poem "Brainstorm," we see a different tension:

> The house was shaken by a rising wind
> That rattled window and door.   He sat alone
> In an upstairs room and heard these things: a blind
> Ran up with a bang, a door slammed, a groan
> Came from some hidden joist, and a leaky tap,
> At any silence of the wind, walked like
> A blind man through the house . . .

Nemerov is equally adept in the lyric mood, and here
too we find that strong opening stroke, the instantaneous perception that begins his "Sunderland," with its Keatsian
echoes:

> It was on a winter's day, as cold, as clear
> As water running underneath the ice,
> Green starwort bending in the water-bed,
> Swayed by invisible power.

The "social muse" (what ever happened to that old
ghost?) is honorably represented with the moving and trenchant "The Murder of William Remington"; but it is more than
a representation, it is another aspect of truth that is everywhere in the poet's world.

> This my modest art
> Brings wilderness well down into the range
> Of any budget . . .

says Nemerov at one point ("The Map-Maker on His Art").
A fair enough credo as worked out by a sensitive writer, always conscious of the poem's purpose, always meeting the
demands of a contemporary intelligence.

7. The Homecoming Game

Reviewed by Charles Poore

Originally published in the "Books of the Times"
column, New York Times, February 28, 1957.
Copyright (c) 1957 by The New York Times Company. Reprinted by permission.

There is a sultry, serpentine heroine in Howard Nemerov's new novel, The Homecoming Game, the likes of which
--or whom--we have not seen since Michael Arlen's potted-
palmy days. Her name is Lily. She gilds what otherwise
might be a story embodying an unlikely collaboration between
Mary McCarthy, Randall Jarrell and the Owen Johnson who
wrote the Lawrenceville stories.

Mr. Nemerov is a graduate of Harvard who now
teaches at Bennington College in Vermont. Two years ago
he received the Kenyon Review Fellowship in Fiction and devoted those distinguished spoils to this babel of variations
on the theme of academic integrity, divergent faiths and the
hope of charity. It is suave, brilliant and entertaining, but
it really does not add up to anything much whatever when all
is said and done.

Sardonic wisdom streaks its pages. Starting with an
antique theme--the plight of the college teacher who has
flunked a star football player the day before the year's most
important game--Mr. Nemerov proceeds to embellish it with
a galvanic lot of dramatizations concerning ethics, intoler-

98

ance, romance, and Lord Acton's suggestions about the corruption that may lie at the heart of power.

The book's hero--not the football hero--is young Prof.
Charles Osman, who teaches history and, sporadically, takes
a long, disquieting view of it.   The athlete under suspension
is Ray Blent, an intelligent undergraduate, rough-hewn though
he may be.   As you will happily foresee, both Charles and
Ray are quickly revealed as men in love with Lily.   The
fact that Lily is an heiress, daughter of a standard-brand
tycoon and college trustee, adds appropriate elements to the
general embroilment.

Mr. Nemerov is not content to let his intricate cha-
rade go at that, however.   He unwinds coils within coils
methodically.   First we see members of the student council
trying to get Charles to change his mind and make Ray eli-
gible to play on a day that may crown him with All-Ameri-
can laurels.

Then Lily takes a hand, and ensnares him with her
ruthlessly cosmopolitan enchantment.   Then, of course,
Charles is called to the college president's office, where the
incumbent fund-raiser and smoother-over makes relaxed suggestions all leading to the popular local notion that if Charles
will reconsider, and at least wait till the game is over to
flunk Ray officially, the greatest good of the greatest possible
number will be served.

And that's not all Charles has to face, by a long
chalk.   In the preliminary grillings he has been allowed to
assume that he alone stands between a dismal homecoming
Saturday game and the potential victory of dear old (Eastern)
Siwash.   Turns out, however, that one more member of the
faculty also failed to give Ray a necessary passing grade.
This other one is a man of resolute and profoundly rooted

indignation. His faith has been held against him by bigots,
his politics has herded him among the little red sheep who
have gone astray.

Now Mr. Nemerov poses for Charles the question
whether he can in time alter his colleague's stanch, explosive views. It will not be enough to get him to clear Ray
by asking him, as Charles does, to identify the color of
Cromwell's horse. Nor are matters speeded forward by the
arrival on the scene of Lily's brusquely indulgent father and
another trustee, a member of the United States Senate whose
portrait Mr. Nemerov does not bother to develop beyond the
timeworn outline of Senator Claghorn.

Well, they all bluster, blandish and horse around in
unsurprising ways until it occurs to Mr. Nemerov to suggest
that the homecoming day football game has been fixed anyway, through the villainous bribery of shady characters bet-
ting roundish sums on the game. When that idea has been
introduced, Mr. Nemerov has a stageful of characters who
are bound to produce fireworks all over the place.

What remains for us, as we read, is the spectacle of
everyone being remarkably fluent if not consistently frank as
the petards are successively hoisted. Although Mr. Nemerov
sometimes bogs down for a page or two at a time in deep-
dish philosophizing, he usually manages to keep things flowing boisterously. The name of Machiavelli is bandied about
at intervals, as I suppose it must be when an academic author is exploring the expediencies that tarnish scholarly integrity.

The campus scene is satirized with an efficiency that
leaves no ivied stone unturned. The most interesting person
present, when all is said and done, is Lily. She is the pre-
siding mistress of these collegiate revels. But where is

Jesting Pilate?

8. A Commodity of Dreams and Other Stories

Reviewed by Martin Tucker

Originally published in Venture, III, Summer 1959.
Reprinted by permission of the author.

Howard Nemerov's most persistent recourse in his
latest book, a collection of stories entitled A Commodity of
Dreams, is to the individual who has been so truncated and
flattened that he has no hopes left. The only thing burning
in him is a guilt complex. In "The Guilty Shall Be Found
Out and Punished," the narrator-hero cannot rid himself of
an itch under the heel of his right foot. The itch is unbear-
able in its reminder of an unspecified guilt. The crime is
never mentioned--the crime is not what the hero has committed but what he has omitted. This bachelor-narrator-
hero, who hides his Daily Mirror under a New York Times,
who stares at women but never advances beyond his lascivi-
ous thoughts, has always managed to live an outwardly respectable life. Now he is being punished for his thoughts--
in his eyes, he is a lecher; he would love to bring his beautiful, coolly possessed secretary into his well-appointed a-
partment and experience with her "a sexual frenzy and bitter, lecherous violence." Finally, his guilt invades his life
until it becomes his mistress. Even in his dreams, the
itch will develop into "fantastic, flowering shapes."
The repressed sexuality in this and other stories is

102

a key to understanding Nemerov's point of view.   The itch,
the naked foot, the erotic imaginings about his secretary--
they are part of that picture of a society in which healthy
sexual expression is lacking.   The result is that Nemerov's
hero finally begins to regard sex as something dirty, tawdry,
prurient--something hidden and belonging to an underworld.
It becomes an itch within his foot, safe in its depths, and
although it cannot be expressed, except covertly, it is at
least owned.

Most of Nemerov's heroes and heroines suffer from
this sense of frustration: the nephew who must not only
"preserve" his dead great-uncle in an outlandish electronic
device in the front parlor but must preside over him every
day and exhaust the fortune he has inherited in doing so;
Harry, Doris, Brewster and Maxine Holladay, who misun-
derstand every honest impulse each of them has so rarely
had; the young man who is possessed of the eye of action
and lacks the eye of knowledge and so endlessly repeats acts
without significance.

The most curious thing, however, in Nemerov's stories is his characters' reaction to impulse.   Almost all of
them are impelled to commit an act of violence.   Their inward rage at some point reaches an impossible scream, and
they explode.   In "A Secret Society," the hero Mr. Pauley
admits his lack of sexual interest in women and men (he
feels it necessary to add the last in describing himself), yet
a few moments later he seizes a gun from a bank guard and
stuffs it in his mouth.   He pulls the trigger, but it doesn't
go off; he has forgotten to release the safety catch.   Even
here, Mr. Pauley feels himself a failure.   Limply, he accepts the arm of his townspeople who carry him off to his
home.

A bachelor, Mr. Pauley is the last descendent of a
well-to-do family in a small industrial town, and he lives
with his spinster sister in an anachronistic mansion. He
feels that the townspeople are secretly laughing at his inef-
fectualness. He wants desperately to feel a part of something but doesn't know how. Most of the time he feels, as
he expresses it, a "wistful tenderness" towards people. He
does not know how to feel anything stronger than that. Characteristically, his one impulse to free himself is through an
act of violence with psycho-sexual overtones, an act which
no one who knows Mr. Pauley as a kindly, gentle middle-
aged bachelor can possibly understand.

This impulse to violence plays the greatest role in
the stories. It serves as the climax to a carefully-wrought
exposition of a repressed individual in a society that is indifferent to him while complaisant about his quirks. In "A
Delayed Hearing," a poor stupid woman driven to paranoia
strikes and kills another woman outside the courtroom where
their case has just been postponed. In "The Amateurs," a
group of neurotic intellectuals bored with their depleted sup-
ply of diversion are shocked when two people--ironically
named Angel (a beautiful sadist) and Hastings (a young man
trying to feel Christ as his personal friend and slow to realize religion is more than a mortal companionship) go forward with the Crucifixion. Their victim dies.

Such an emphasis on pain and despair is bound to
pall unless the artist can present his view with a profundity
that enables the sameness of his theme to be shown in all
its various guises and facets. Kafka is no less despairing
than Nemerov, yet he is not depressing finally. More important, Kafka is aggressively hopeless while Nemerov is
blatantly weary. The difference lies in the broader view

that Kafka takes.   Nemerov's stories remain personal case
histories whereas Kafka's fiction becomes allegorical.

This lack of total immersion may spring from Nemerov's own sincere, bitter withdrawal from the painful attri-
tion of human hopes and desires he so clearly exposes.   For
it is no exaggeration to say that all his heroes and heroines
feel like frauds.   In "The Ocean to Cynthia," two are actually fraudulent, a fake priest and a false lover.   Their
names reveal them, for Father Frank is the most deceptive
priest around, while Mr. Bower is a sentimentalist who can
offer no shelter to any woman he seduces.   Between them
stands another symbolically-named character, Elizabeth
Brayle, who cannot read the secret of life in any language.
In "Yore," the story closest to a complete allegory, all the
characters know they are hiding from reality because "reality is always improbable."   Instead, they seek out romance
and go to cafes like the Forgeterie in the Hotel Beauldvoir
(an anagram for beautiful old view?).   Unable to face life,
they pass the time away in conjuring up the past.   Yet all
of them know, in the moment of their declaration for the
preference of romance, that reality is breathing over their
shoulders.   The days of "Yore" are over, no matter how
hard they cling to the past.

This romantic attachment to the past is another feature of Nemerov's work.   In "Yore," he satirizes the feeling while showing the poignancy of the loss of a tradition
that told men what to believe and where to fight.   In "A
Secret Society," his hero yearns for its womb-like comfort.
In "A Sorcerer's Eye," still another hero cries out tragical-
ly for those days when the ignorance of childhood saved one
from the emptiness of adulthood.   In Nemerov's most successful story, "A Commodity of Dreams," the theme is car-

ried to its limit.   Here, the hero catalogues his dreams and
opens a "museum" in his attempt to freeze alive the past.

　　　The important thing however is not the reliance of his
characters on the past, but the sense of the past's betrayal
of them.   In every story, it is the past which has deserted
the characters; the past has left them high and dry in the in-
choate moment of the present.   This point of view repre-
sents a sensitive writer's comment on the modern world's
lack of engagement, its passivity, its cold denial of any unusual or oddball individual.   The statement carries pathos
and poignancy, but its context lacks the tragedy of a major
outcry, principally because Nemerov has not objectified his
characters into more than personal symbols.   What he has
done is a more minor (though important accomplishment: he
has turned symbols into transient literary characters.

9.   New and Selected Poems

Reviewed by Ambrose Gordon, Jr.

It is perhaps a mistake to review one's friends; necessarily one is prejudiced, and in all sorts of queer ways. Doubly so for the friends of one's youth.   Admiration, nostalgia, expectations perhaps not fulfilled, or fulfilled differently from what one had expected, get in the way, obscure the accomplishment, blind the eye, set one to dreaming.   So for this review of Howard Nemerov's New & Selected Poems, a volume at least partly retrospective, containing as it does, in addition to fifteen new poems, selections from four earlier volumes: The Image and the Law (1947), Guide to the Ruins (1950), The Salt Garden (1955), and Mirrors and Windows (1958).   The accomplishment is real and great, but how to define it?

It is notorious that poets prefer always their most recent work, friends usually their earlier.   How could it be otherwise?   Let the present reviewer at least try to be explicit about his prejudices.   Mr. Nemerov was the first of my contemporaries that I read--almost the first modern poet I had read.   The excitement I can still remember and it very likely colors or clouds my judgment.   One's own youth

is still caught up and alive in the cherished lines; how could
later, and more expert, poetry ever please as much?

This review is concerned, then, with the now and the
then, as--happily--so are the poems themselves. With the
then rather less than the now. I take my text from the first
poem of the present volume, entitled "Moment":

> Under the arc-lights where the sentry walks
> His lonely wall it never moves from now,
> The crying in the cell is also now,
> And now is quiet in the tomb as now
> Explodes inside the sun, and it is now
> In the saddle of space, where argosies of dust
> Sail outward blazing, and the mind of God,
> The flash across the gap of being, thinks
> In the instant absence of forever: now.

The lines are arresting, beautiful, and a bit frightening;
rendering the flash of consciousness across a synapse in the
brain, or across the gap of being. Now. Yet such momen-
taneity becomes in another poem a glimpse of the absurd by
Mr. Nemerov's shifting the focus ever so slightly:

> A peels an apple, while B kneels to God,
> C telephones to D, who has a hand
> On E's knee, F coughs, G turns up the sod
> For H's grave, I do not understand
> But J is bringing one clay pigeon down
> While K brings down a nightstick on L's head . . .

Many of Mr. Nemerov's poems in one way or another are
about "now"--as might be suggested by a sampling of first
lines: "Now, starflake frozen on the windowpane," "The
place is forgotten now . . ." "A misty heat, now that the
spring has gone," "Now as the year turns toward its darkness." And there are others.

Out of the now and the then one may construct a
world--many worlds. The resulting patterns in Mr. Nemerov's poems range from simple elegy to much more compli-

cated arrangements, corresponding, as he tells us, to two
different ways of looking at the world.

> But what I thought today, that made me cry,
> Is this, that we live in two kinds of thing:
> The powerful trees, thrusting into the sky
> Their black patience, are one, and that branching
> Relation teaches how we endure and grow;
>   The other is the snow,
> Falling in a white chaos from the sky,
> As many as the sands of all the seas . . .

A relatively simple elegy like "The Remorse for Time"
might be likened to the patterns formed in a pool of still
water by two stones dropped--call them "then" and "now"--,
their crossed and crossing circles forming the poem, "a
kind of reticulation regular and of simple origins." This is
the way the world appears to the temporal, sublunary eye:
the pathos of time suffered, change endured, childhood gone,
youth lost.

> But if you throw a handful of sand into the water, it
>   is confusion,
> Not because the same laws have ceased to obtain, but
>   only because
> The limits of your vision in time and number forbid
>   you to discriminate
> Such fine, quick, myriad events as the angels and
>   archangels, thrones
> And dominations, principalities and powers, are
>   delegated to witness
> And declare the glory of before the Lord of everything
>   that is.
> Of these great beings and mirrors of being, little at
>   present is known,
> And of the manner of their perceiving not much more.
>   We imagine them
> As benign, as pensively smiling and somewhat coldly
>   smiling, but
> They may not be as we imagine them.

The former, and simpler, type of poem is characteristically
dominated by images of water; the other by images of trees,

twisted roots, seeds, vines, veins--by patterns of snowflakes, particularly by snow.

> White water now in the snowflake's prison,
> A mad king in a skullcap thinks these thoughts
> In regular hexagons, each one unlike
> Each of the others.

Of this latter sort, "Runes" and "The Scales of the Eyes"
are the most ambitious, and at the same time the most fully
achieved, examples; poems visionary, deliberately complex
and cold, like a scene glimpsed by winter lightning.   So
(Mr. Nemerov tells us) must the poet

> . . . from his wintry heart
> And in the lightning second's sight,
> Illuminate this dream
>   With a cold art.

What are the forms the coldness takes?   There are
the expected scenes of ice and snow registered by the poet
who has spent more than a decade in Vermont (except for a
year's questionable respite in Minnesota): the storm windows,
the frosty pane, the children skating, the snowy cobwebbing
of winter trees, farmers cutting great blocks of ice from a
pond, grey skies, and so on.   But poets choose their landscape and their weather, these wintry glimpses being clearly the outward and visible signs of an inward and spiritual
chill--a deliberately cultivated chill.   And more important
than the content, there is the form itself.   The predominant-
ly ten-syllable lines have achieved an extraordinary poise;
the reader is never rushed, and is seldom swept along:

> People are putting up storm windows now,
> Or were, this morning, until the heavy rain
> Drove them indoors.   So, coming home at noon,
> I saw storm windows lying on the ground
> Frame-full of rain; through the water and glass
> I saw the crushed grass, how it seemed to stream

> Away in lines like seaweed on the tide
> Or blades of wheat leaning under the wind.

Beautiful, and beautifully framed: the streaming waters
caught between glass, caught at the moment that is now, at
the eternal noon. Necessarily arrested, necessarily static.
There are many such images and many such poems. Taken
either together or separately each line is beautiful; each different, each the same, as snowflakes are different and the
same. What one perhaps misses is a force thrusting through
the poem from line to line; the end-stopped, or semi-end-
stopped, verses do not gather up and shove; they remain
poised, crystallized, at rest.

The characteristic mode of Mr. Nemerov's later poems is meditation--not drama, and only secondarily narra-
tive--and to my mind they include some of the best meditative verse of our time. "The Pond" is a notable example.
Yet the very detachment creates a curiously dreamlike meditation. We are told, in that poem, of the little boy Chris-
topher's death soberly:

> There was a tragedy, if that is what
> One calls it, the newspapers called it that:
> "Pond Claims First Victim" (it still had no name),
> As though a monster underneath the ice
> Had been in wait to capture the little boy
> Skating in darkness all alone, away
> From the firelight--the others heard his cry
> But he was gone before they found the place--

The lines are quietly compassionate and controlled; and yet
at times one wonders whether Mr. Nemerov has not achieved
his quiet perfection at too great a cost. As with the master
Yeats, Howard Nemerov's "cold art" appears to have been
deliberately cultivated--it is an acquired characteristic.
Compare the beautiful opening stanza of "On the Flight into
Egypt," written when the poet was twenty:

> At night, the insects on my window-pane
> Trouble me.   Why should there be
> Such batterings as the bluster of their wings
> Against the window? Why, not half the kings
> Of Spain made such a beating and a battering
> With the withered wings of their robes
> Over kingdoms in Hungary or Heaven.

The later verse is certainly finer art; yet it is by comparison numbed; the emotions are deeper but the sensibility has
retrenched and hardened; the moment is arrested; everything
is lying ominously in wait; nothing happens.   The little boy
remains forever skating away through the darkness.   And indeed, many of the later poems--the more meditative at
least--are, as it were, not so much seen and felt as
dreamed.

> That is my theme, of thought and the defeat
> Of thought before its object, where it turns
> As from a mirror, and returns to be
> The thought of something and the thought of thought,
> A trader doubly burdened, commercing
> Out of one stillness and into another.

There is always the stillness, the now, the point of arrest.

Argal?   Advice.   It is always an impertinence, but
is said to be the prerogative of reviewers.   Mr. Nemerov
is today, I believe, one of the most accomplished of practicing poets.   He can do, apparently, anything.   Indeed the
range of his poems is far wider than I have suggested.   He
is one of the wittiest poets we have and certainly one of the
most intelligent.   I wish, though, that he would escape from
the very beautiful prison of meditation, his salt garden, his
snowflake prism.   I wish, for example, that he might try a
long narrative or dramatic poem, for various voices and in
varied measures (eschewing the pentameter).   Then the promise hinted at in his "Sleeping Beauty" would, I think, be fulfilled:

This ends only with a kiss, the story said.
Then all the snoring barons will arise
And the dogs begin to bark, the king and queen
Order their coach and four--all on a kiss
The whole world will begin to happen again,
People will yawn, stretch, begin to forget
Whatever they dreamed that was so like a dream.

10. The Next Room of the Dream

a) Reviewed by Hayden Carruth

Originally published as "Interim Report," Poetry, September 1963. Reprinted by permission of the author and Poetry. Copyright 1963 by The Modern Poetry Association.

Half of this book is taken up by two verse plays on Biblical themes, and since I'm not qualified to discuss them, I'll pass them over; remarking only that the language seems to me nearly successful, but not quite; it lacks the vivacity or tone which we want from dramatic verse, even when the plays are, like these, reflective in intent. But the other considerations of structure, pace, theatrical expediency, etc., I must leave to critics of the stage, though I earnestly recommend these two plays as excellent texts for their attention.

The rest of the book consists of short poems, most of which are wisecracks. For my purpose here, I define the wisecrack as a poem of wit in which the two parts fail to cohere. A proper conceit, as we know, consists of a joke and a moral; they must resist each other fiercely yet remain locked together--a sort of terrified embrace; and when they fall apart the joke becomes merely a joke, the moral becomes merely a platitude. Which is what happens in too many of Nemerov's poems. Why? When I reviewed his last book, I said flatly it was a defect of meter and let

it go at that, and my friends chided me, quite justly, for
being so short with a fine poet.   Nemerov has a good ear
for all verbal effects, as we know from his best earlier
work; for example, that much-anthologized piece about the
lady and the whale.   There meter does what it should; it
fixes the tone of voice, emphasis, and ultimately the meaning of the poem.   Meter is, after all, what makes any artifice of language come alive, and I hope it's clear I'm not
talking about metronomic or syllable-counting techniques.
Nemerov's verse is far from these; his meter is varied and
flexible; but I still think that in his recent work his metri-
cal effects have become rather mechanical, rather predict-
able and repetitious.   We recognize Nemerov all right, but
a Nemerov who is copying his own manner by rote, turning
the stuff out too easily and slickly.   The general tone be-
trays fatigue; and the result is a meter which fails to do its
work, fails to sustain and consolidate the feeling, in Nemerov's case the feeling--verve, élan--of wit in a forcing moral action.   It isn't always a failure; there's a poem in this
book, "At a Country Hotel," which is close to the whale poem in excellence, perhaps good enough to become a new anthology piece.   But one poem will not support a book.   The
reviewer does not inquire, of course, into the deeper cause
of a technical failure, especially in the case of a poet as
gifted as Nemerov.   One can only wish him, as I and I'm
sure all readers do, the best of luck, and assure him we
will wait for his next book with every anticipation of re-
newed enjoyment.

b)   Reviewed by W. R. Johnson

We are all friends here and must sometimes speak
plainly.   Let us start with my plain assertion that Howard
Nemerov is the best poet practicing these days and that these
are the best poems being published.   Let us take the occasion of this book, forty-eight new poems and two new plays,
to speak of him and of his work as if we happened to be
passing an evening together and he happened to be somewhere else.

Listen to a few lines:

Now I can see certain simplicities
In the darkening rust and tarnish of the time,
And say over the certain simplicities,
The running water and the standing stone,
The yellow haze of the willow and the black
Smoke of the elm, the silver, silent light
Where suddenly, readying toward nightfall,
The sumac's candelabrum darkly flames.

With this in our ear let us recall that we were a
Donne-struck generation, and he the most generic.   Remember some undergraduate lines of his, about a snapshot:

I doubt it is a parable of time:
How love can make an angle with the sun
To trap time on a page, forcing the same
To other time, and without running, run.

But I alone, and you in this flat land
Remain.   That time and place you have abstracted
Will turn and die upon my turning hand:
With twice dying, time has some price extracted.

We were taught to loathe, but how thoroughly and lovingly

we learned to loathe Shelley, Tennyson. It took a while of
reading and imitating and analyzing for us to invent a centri-
fuge for the Quartets and words to substitute for "whee"
when we read Yeats. It was Yeats, mainly, who lifted us
out of that stage where, to start a poem, one cast around
for a solid image with a good ambiguity and then turned the
hand-organ's crank.

But however many rooms have been added to our
dream since James was King, poetry for us (with prose and
painting and love and science) has always had to consist of
magic, of the healing of the sick or the destruction of the
enemy or the pleasing of the beloved or the conquering of
death by a deliberate manipulation of ordinary unsanctified
objects, never by prayer. Never by prayer, which is to say
that our only faith has been and is in metaphysical poetry.

Nemerov now seldom speaks with the phrases of Mar-
vell or Donne, and he yokes his images in less violent ways.
Turn in your book to page 6, "To the Mannequins":

> Adorable images
> Plaster of Paris
> Lilies of the field,
> You are not alive, therefore
> Pathos will be out of place.
> But I have learned
> A fact about your fate,
> And it is this:
> After you go out of fashion
> Beneath your many fashions,
> Or when your elbows and knees
> Have been bruised powdery white,
> So that you are no good to anybody . . .

Having explicitly forsworn the pathetic fallacy, the speaker
is not really cheating to mention the elbows and knees as
bruised, thus diffidently evoking the pathos of, say, char-
women. And it is within the rules to continue:

> They will take away your gowns,
> Your sables and bathing suits,
> Leaving exposed before all men
> Your inaccessible bellies
> And pointless nubilities.

Those bellies are literally inacessible.   The inanimate nu-
bilities are literally pointless (to fit a Cup D brassiere).
And furthermore there is no outrageous mixing of degrees of
abstraction in the images, cf. "how love can make an angle
with the sun"; the speaker has his own vocabulary.   He goes
on:

> Movers will come by night
> And load you into trucks
> And take you away to the Camps,
> Where soldiers, or the State Police,
> Will use you as targets
> For small arms practice,
> Leading me to inquire,
> Since pathos is out of place,
> What it is that they are practicing.

This is a very metaphysical poem, and when all the harmon-
ics of that last image-less line have registered in the sound-
ing chamber of the mind, it turns out to be about a Metaphysical Problem.   What is our relation with these effigies,
anyway?

Howard's first novel, The Rock, was about a town
living beneath one of those balancing boulders that may fall
at any moment and squash it.   But it goes on being a town;
each human pursuit, each coupling and combining of people,
each communal enterprise is normal though intrinsically modified, qualified, informed by the Rock.   It was a situation
within a conceit, the sort that might have been used by Donne
for a sermon or by Melville for a story.   For its telling it
required the tone of voice, the manner of a narrator somewhere between the preaching Donne and the diarizing Mel-

ville. The result, as I recall across seventeen years, was
dramatic: a narrator who was the Chorus of the piece, one
of its players, a citizen of the town who yet spoke as the
escort of the audience. He has become the speaker in most
of Nemerov's poems, and most of them are scenes or tab-
leaux of the town under the Rock--its galleries, stores,
power houses, playing children, private detectives, thwarted
lovers, unthwarted lovers, statues, board meetings, tele-
phones, schools, and the streams and fields and woods on its
outskirts. The narrator of these poems, the Chorus of these
pieces, always stays on stage, so to speak. The imple-
ments of magic employed by him or through him are only
the properties and lighting and characters of the sets themselves. For Nemerov the limitation of the method is advan-
tageous, since he practices using a stage set for Mae West
to give his audience Cleopatra.

Not all audiences like it, especially those who prefer
prayer to magic and money to art. Years ago a lady agent
of the literary squad on Madison Avenue ticked off some
work that Nemerov and a friend were trying to sell for eat-
ing-money as "contrived and mechanical--no heart." Recently a lady agent of the morals squad in roughly the same part
of town went into print concerning one of the poems in this
book: "The mean hypocrisy of certain intellectual faddists
seeking to destroy our most beautiful holiday traditions is
typified. . . by a single word in the poem 'Santa Claus' by
Howard Nemerov in the Christmas 1962 issue of The Reporter magazine . . . . 'Played at the better stores by bums,
for money,' writes Howard Nemerov, 'this annual savior of
the economy speaks in the parables of the dollar sign . . . .'
Is the man a bum who plays Santa Claus where you trade?
. . . It seems to me that it is some self-appointed de-

bunkers of Christmas who urgently require debunking. Writing for money, they enjoy many goodies of the prosperous
American economy which, at Christmas time, makes available to consumers the goods manufactured "thruout" the year
by millions of working men and women. Moreover, celebra-
tion of the holiday season gives employment to several hundred
thousand extra part-time workers who are thus enabled to
add much needed earnings to the annual family income . . .
Permit me to repeat my question: "Are the men 'bums' who
play Santa Claus in the better stores and charitable organi-
zations of your community? . . . "

     This is, as it claims to be, the authentic Voice (as
they say at MLA) of the American culture, for its author is
Alice Widener, Publisher, U. S. A. Magazine. I vouch for it
in spite of the disturbing use of the term "workers" and the
slightly deviationist implication of that crack about extra
earnings being "much needed." It is authentic and hostile.
I expect Miss or Mrs. Widener will protest to her congressman when she learns that Howard Nemerov has been ap-
pointed Congress's Poet in Residence of Congress's Library
at Congress's constituents' expense. But I trust that the
congressman will take our expert word for it that Nemerov
really is the best poet writing today and really does adorn
American Culture as we intellectual faddists seek to continue
it even though he may not entirely embody the American culture.

     In any event his position in the culture is a serious
one, a responsible one, for his work, as we said, is the
practice of magic, and a magician in any culture is the fellow who rattles some sticks and makes it rain, while he
hears the spirits of the tribe in his secret ear. He is the
man whose pots and figurines, when set in just the right pat-

tern by his practicing hand, recreate the tribe's creation
and explain death.

How this magic works without conjury is a subject
for essays, long Critical Essays of which there will undoubt-
edly be plenty in times to come. His own comments on the
making of it are in the closing lines of the last poem ("Lion
& Honeycomb"), just before the plays in this book:

> So much coffee and so many cigarettes,
> Gone down the drain, gone up in smoke,
> Just for the sake of getting something right
> Once in a while, something that could stand
> On its own flat feet to keep out windy time
> And the worm, something that might simply be,
> Not as the monument in the smoky rain
> Grimly endures, but that would be
> Only a moment's inviolable presence,
> The moment before disaster, before the storm,
> In its peculiar silence, an integer
> Fixed in the middle of the fall of things,
> Perfected and casual as to a child's eye
> Soap bubbles are, and skipping stones.

How wonderful it is to read these cadences. How properly
epigraphic are these lines to Howard's work.

11. Poetry and Fiction: Essays

a) Reviewed by Louis D. Rubin, Jr.

Originally published as "Well Worth the Saying."
Kenyon Review, Spring 1964. Reprinted by permission of the author.

When Howard Nemerov's most recent book of poems,
The Next Room of the Dream, was published last year, one
reviewer quoted some lines from the book, compared them
with some of Nemerov's earliest published work, and concluded that as a poet Nemerov had come a long way. So he
has. The better poems in the recent book differ sharply
from the verse that he was publishing back in the middle and
late 1940's.

I mention this because in the preface to this collection of critical essays, his first such, Nemerov begins by
saying something that is markedly different from the usual
line that is handed out by poets and novelists on such occasions. "Poetry and criticism," he declares, "are as a
double star, and if we wish to go on in poetry beyond the
first ecstatic stirrings of the imagination . . . we shall do
well to learn all we can of what poetry is and try to see by
means of many examples how the art is constantly redefin-
ing itself. Studying one's contemporaries, one gets an idea
of what is possible, as well as many ideas of what is not."
Reading through these prose pieces, one realizes that this is
precisely what Nemerov has been doing, and that in part, at
122

least, this is what accounts for the fact that, unlike many
another poet whose work began to be talked about in the immediate postwar years, Nemerov's technique has been steadily developing and changing. With each new volume of verse
he has expanded his range and clarified his style.

This unabashed willingness to write criticism, and to
assert categorically that to do so is not only worth-while but
even highly important, goes along with an attitude that one
finds expressed throughout Nemerov's criticism. This is,
that poetry is a highly important kind of knowledge, "no
mere playing with the counters of meaning, but a perpetual
re-deriving of the possibility of meaning from matter, of the
intelligible world from the brute recalcitrance of things."
Now, when one has this attitude, and can believe in the
depths of his being that poetry is unique and essential, one
will not fear to write or read criticism. Those poets, and
there are many of them, who are constantly complaining a-
bout the tyranny of the critics, and who view criticism as a
menace to the integrity and the writing of poetry, only reveal thereby their underlying doubt of the importance of poetry. In actuality, criticism is always subordinate to poetry, and exists only in order to understand and to confirm
the poetry. When Karl Shapiro, for example, writes that
"changes in taste are brought about by critics," he is talking entire nonsense. It was not Eliot's critical essays that
"created" modern poetry, or Pound's, either; it was "Prufrock" and The Waste Land that did it. The preface to the
Lyrical Ballads did not end neoclassicism in English verse;
the Lyrical Ballads themselves did so. Good poetry has repeatedly shown its ability to outlast hostile criticism, to
force criticism to accommodate itself to the dimensions of
new poetry. While the dominant criticism of any day has

customarily shown itself hostile to really important changes
in poetry, in the long run the poetry has always won out.

It is the realization that this is so, that the poem is
so much more influential and more seminal than its criticism, that makes Nemerov unafraid to write criticism. He
does not, in short, fear to think long and hard about poetry;
he is sufficiently confident of the value of poetry not to believe that thinking about it might interfere with writing it.

The taste reflected in these essays is quite catholic;
he can deal with poets as diverse as Robert Graves and W.
H. Auden, as Theodore Roethke and Karl Shapiro, and find
something to admire in each of them. Not iconoclastic by
principle, he is nevertheless no respecter of reputations.
A case in point, which many will remember, is his excellent review essay, first published in The Sewanee Review
in 1959, of Wallace Fowlie's translation of St.-John Perse's
Seamarks. In this essay he came out and said what many
had felt, but nobody had been willing to say, which was that
when one got past the highly attractive printing and binding
of the Bollingen editions of Perse, and the blurbs by distinguished men of letters, and one examined the poetry itself,
there was relatively little there beyond a great deal of By-
ronic posturing and some competent naming of objects. As
Nemerov said of one inflated passage, "the expressions
themselves are some of them literal and some figurative;
taking them singly, we might find some good and others bad,
depending on the context, but their combined aim seems to
be to bludgeon us into submission by the tasteless filling up
of a monotonously repeated form . . . ."

Likewise Nemerov looked at Dylan Thomas, in an essay published in The Kenyon Review in 1953 when the Thomas boom was at its peak. He found, as many others have

since concluded now that the force of Thomas' own personality reading the poems aloud no longer dominates the imagination, that in many of the poems, including some of the
best-known ones, there is much rhapsodizing, a great deal
of gesturing, but with so little control throughout that "the
tension and sinuosity are lost, and the energetic impulsion
which begins the line either cracks up or proceeds as shout-
ing; nor does any intensification of assonance and so forth
overcome this difficulty." Thomas' vaunted talent for bold
metaphor, he said, is gaudy, arbitrary, and ultimately self-
defeating. Though Thomas wrote some fine poems, especially toward the last, the bulk of his work is characteristically
empty and rhetorical. As Nemerov says, "the art of sink-
ing in poetry is not dead; and there is the art of rising,
too, like a paper bag in a high wind."

More typically, Nemerov writes to praise excellence
rather than to deflate reputations. He is at his best with
Wallace Stevens; there are two pieces on Stevens, of which
the second, "The Bread of Faithful Speech--Wallace Stevens
and the Voices of Imagination," is one of the best statements of just how a skillful poet addresses his subject that
I have ever read. There are excellent essays on John
Crowe Ransom, Allen Tate, Robert Graves, and Reed Whittemore. Weldon Kees's work receives an expert appreciation. There is even a good essay on Henry Wadsworth Longfellow, in which Nemerov demonstrates not only a good his-
torical sense but the ability to recognize and appraise good
verse when it is not at all like his own kind of poetry.

In the general essays, Nemerov's chief theme seems
to be the defense of poetry against charges of its unimpor-
tance. Thus he takes pains to show the differences between
the approaches of art and institutionalized religion, only to

conclude that what art offers is just the kind of revelation
of the world that religion offers, but "by vision and not by
dogma." At another point, in a most moving discussion of
what poetry has been for himself and his fellow poets, he
distinguishes between the impulse to write and the desire to
be widely read: "When something comes to you to be dealt
with according to such skill and energy as you may have to
give it," he declares, "you give it what you have; which may
not be much, or nearly enough, but excludes for the time
all thought of whether it will be acceptable to 'the public'--
an entity, I repeat, of which poets have very little opportunity of forming an image." Granted then, that the desire
to write well has nothing to do with practical usefulness, he
says, it remains true that "a new inflection of the voice may
be the seed of new mind, new character, and many persons
still to be born will enact in their lives the poet's word.
Ours is a power the more immense for not being directed
to a specific or immediate end other than the poem itself."
And he concludes, "we write, at last, because life is hopeless and beautiful."

There are so many good and informative essays and
essay-reviews in this collection that one can do little more
than describe the contents. Though chiefly a poet, Nemerov
has much to say about prose fiction--he has, after all, published two novels and a volume of short stories. His discussion of the form of the short novel sets forth the virtues
of that genre most invitingly. He has a special fondness
for Vladimir Nabokov and Thomas Mann, and there are two
excellent pieces on each of them. He reprints his diagnos-
is, for The Nation of November 2, 1957, of James Gould
Cozzens' By Love Possessed, which many will recall as having been, along with Dwight MacDonald's review in Commen-

tary, instrumental in restoring the literary world to sanity
upon that occasion. And there is also a remarkable thematic analysis of Faulkner's Light in August. Turning to criticism, a review of Stanley Edgar Hyman's The Armed Vision
presents that explosive critique of critics in all its flawed
contentiousness. Two books on Shakespeare are properly
classified and castigated. (Earlier in the book there is an
ingenious defense of The Two Gentlemen of Verona, in which
Nemerov almost, but not quite, convinces the reader, and
himself, that the play is better than he knows it really is.)

Written over the course of fifteen years, these es-
says--to return, finally, to the business of poets and their
writing of literary criticism--are not conceptual in form,
which is to say that they demonstrate no particular mode of
criticism, no elaborate theoretical structure upon which to
arrange critiques of stories and poems as if they were test
cases for a specific method. Rather, they are generally informative in nature, the product of Nemerov's continuing poetic education, and they offer us the opportunity to watch a
talented and intelligent poet as he deals with various kinds
of literature. They are marked by good sense, an unswerv-
ing belief in the necessity for close reading, a conviction of
the ultimate worth of imaginative literature, and the unity
that comes from the internal consistency of a good mind.
His book is the kind to which one can return again and a-
gain, always with the confidence that what is said will be
said well, and be well worth the saying.

b) Reviewed by Herbert Weisinger

I must confess that, though I had known Howard Nemerov's poems and novels and had read them with pleasure,
I was not aware of the extent and variety of his literary
criticism. Now, with the collection of his essays, lectures,
and reviewed in Poetry and Fiction: Essays, it is clear
that his is a critical voice deserving of an attentive and ap-
preciative audience.

The 37 pieces in this volume were written between
1948-62 and are arranged, not in the order of composition,
but by literary forms: the first and third sections being
concerned with general questions of poetry and fiction, the
second and fourth with discussions of specific examples of
the two forms, and the final group consisting of analyses of
the problems of translation. The bulk of the book, being
made up in the main of reviews of the work of recent writers, is contemporary in orientation, but there are also longer essays on classic writers: Dante, Shakespeare, Byron,
Longfellow, and Mann.

Nemerov is neither a literary historian nor an es-
thetician nor a systematizer, and he belongs to no school of
literary criticism. With one exception, all the pieces are
concerned with specific problems of literature and with specific pieces of work. The one exception is the essay, "The
Dream of Reason," a powerful attack from the point of view
of liberal humanism on the kind of genetic engineering advo-
cated by Hermann J. Muller, and, by implication, on the

pretensions of certain scientists. On the evidence of this
paper I had hoped for more essays on larger social questions, but Nemerov sticks to his last.

As a literary historian, I found the way in which he
goes about his work fascinating since it differs so much from
mine. I tend to approach a work of literature from the outside, so to speak, in terms of its category, structure, and
social and intellectual ambience. I bring to bear on it information and attitudes derived from extra-literary sources,
from literary history, linguistics, the history of ideas, psychology, anthropology, and the like. In other words, I close
in on the work by coming up on it along several avenues of
approach.

Nemerov, on the other hand, writes from inside the
work outward; he is concerned with the nuances of tones and
textures; above all, he is most attentive to the act of making. He writes, in short, as a practicing poet and novelist
confronting the same problems of craft which have occupied
the poet or novelist he is examining. Though he is too po-
lite to say so, I would guess that he finds my way exasper-
atingly quite beside the point. And I would suspect that is
why he reacted so strongly against Stanley Edgar Hyman's
The Armed Vision, which takes as its thesis the function of
literary criticism as "the organized use of non-literary techniques and bodies of knowledge to obtain insights into literature."

I have no intention of arguing the merits of one or
the other way of proceeding to the examination and evalua-
tion of a work of literature; the ideal literary critic should
be able to do both and to do more: to fuse them in a single,
yet comprehensive, critical tool. Unfortunately, such critics
have been, and are, rare indeed, and we must do what we

can as the bent of our temperaments and training directs us,
only hoping that we have enough modesty and sense to know
when we fall short and need help.

There is, therefore, no point in trying to place Nemerov in the correct critical file tagged with the correct critical label. Rather, we have to deduce from the body of his
work the guidelines of his thinking, to generalize from his
practice his principles of criticism. One way of doing this
is to enter the names of the writers he considers in the appropriate credit and debit columns of his critical ledger.

On the credit side of the ledger we find the poets
Stevens, Ransom, Tate, Graves, Whittemore and Kees; the
novelists Nabokov, Sillitoe and Mann; and the critics Blackmur and those students of Shakespeare who use the method
of image, symbol and myth analysis. On the debit side we
find the poets MacLeish, Viereck, Spender, Jarrell, Roethke,
Shapiro, Winters, Dylan Thomas, and Perse, and possibly
Auden; the novelists Cozzens, Warren, Herbert Gold, and
possibly Faulkner; and the critics Cowley, Vivas, and Hyman.
To continue, but to vary the financial figure, Nemerov holds
a distinctively personal portfolio; his interest in the critical
market is neither in the quick buck of speculative promo-
tions nor in safe institutional growth stock, but in the pleasure of the exercise of his own independent taste and judgment.

I have said that Nemerov is concerned with the act of
making. It is making of a special kind which moves him
and for which he looks, however, and I would define it as
poetry which is intensely self-aware of itself as poetry and
which glows with a special élan and excitement when it finds
its own solutions to its own problems. "I would hold," he
writes, "that there is, in addition to the emotion dealt with

by poetry, an emotion of poetry and alone proper to it, a
rhythmic or patterned exaltation which takes up and trans-
forms its complex material of feelings and objects, making
them dance in a different and noneditorial world, of which,
despite the seriousness and sadness of its themes, the dom-
inating traits are gaiety, energy, and control."

The hallmark of Nemerov's criticism, then, is intense self-awareness, as it is, I believe, of his poetry and
fiction as well. It is an awareness so conscious that it
takes its greatest pleasure and pride in the consciousness of
that awareness; it is constantly seeing itself see itself, constantly sharpening its sight. The result is an attitude of
mind sophisticated and wry, concerned, not with storming
the ramparts of earth and heaven, but with finding elegant
solutions to problems so difficult technically that only those
who know how difficult they really are know how really elegant are the solutions.

Wonderfully skilled, knowledgeable and cultivated,
Nemerov is a conspicuous exemplar of the man of letters of
our time. Yet there is lacking a certain dedication, a certain passion; devotion to the art of poetry is, after all, not
quite the same as devotion to poetry. I am not trying to be
superior; devotion to the study of literature is not devotion
to literature either. We neither of us--and all the rest of
like mind--dares great things, partly because we do not have
the temperament, partly because we do not know what great
things are in the context of our times, but mostly because
we know in advance they will be in vain.

I occasionally envy men who are completely unself-
conscious, who never look over their shoulders, who move
directly from thought to deed, who accomplish things. But
when I consider what they have accomplished, and more,

what those accomplishments have cost, then I think that we who are haunted by self-awareness have our achievements too.   And I would point to Nemerov's Poetry and Fiction as an example and measure of our kind of accomplishment.

12.   Journal of the Fictive Life

Reviewed by E. J. Schulze

The occasion of this latest book by Howard Nemerov
is a crisis in his personal and professional life.   He feels
"almost a compulsion" to write a novel, but he cannot, somehow, do it: he has trouble with beginnings--too many ideas,
either trite or unbelievable ideas.   He suggests that the root
of his "compulsion" and of his paralysis is the same, a "secret" of his personality, something buried in the details of
his own life that blocks his energies and simultaneously
presses on his consciousness.   The novel that will not come,
that indeed, he both needs and secretly does not want to
happen or to have written, is the intimate story of his own
life.

To put it simply, the Journal of the Fictive Life is
the intimate account of himself that Nemerov has refused
and still refuses to give in a novel, as fiction.   He suffers,
he tells us early in the book, from a fear of betraying his
friends, his family, his reputation, and from a reticence to
expose himself indecorously to a public he has only recently
acquired, mostly through his poetry--especially the fine volume Mirrors and Windows.   He writes: "after seven books,

133

I was absolutely neglected; then, it began to happen, and
now, after ten books, I am practically a pillar of the church,
or ruined temple of poetry."

Yet, his wish not to betray, not to be disloyal, is
complex. It finds relief in a definition of the novel as "a
disclosure of secrets," and in the perception that "at a certain age, theory takes over," that it is good and necessary
for a writer to "think seriously about his art." Instead of
writing his novel, then, Nemerov writes about his novel;
instead of betraying himself and others, he writes about the
"act of betrayal," and especially about the way the mind "be-
trays itself" by concealing its true sources of humiliation
and embarrassment. He has turned his fear into a duty, a
moral and artistic task. Yet, he is also very much aware
of the irony of his self-consciousness: "perhaps . . . self-
examination, analysis, all production of general ideas, thought
itself, are in the end evasions of a story."

A strong but gentle irony characterizes almost all of
his attempts to deal with the interrelationships of life and
fiction, his major theme. The Journal seems to be an elaborate and serious double entendre, built on the metaphor
that "life is a story." The credibility of the metaphor itself frees him to steal from either of its sides to explain
the other. Hence, if a story is "a disclosure of secrets,"
and those secrets betray the guilt of living persons (particularly the author's), then art itself may have "secret meanings" which a self-examination by the artist might reveal.
The conclusion reached by this logic is both interesting and
inevitable: the "secret meanings" of art equal the "character" of the artist.

It is the artist's character (or guilty personality),
the life that yields to the scrutiny of imagination, that is

defined by the phrase, "the fictive life." It is a life at
once connected with and opposed to the life of fictional characters. In both "lives" the imagination treats details, whatever their source: dreams, romances, sensations, memo-
ries, novels. The imagination produces and makes significant the circumstances necessary to belief. Yet, the "lives"
are also clearly opposed to one another; the fictive life exposes art; the lively fiction conceals it.

The journal of this fictive, real-myth life thus pur-
sues two tracks at once. One leads to personality, and dis-
closes the secrets of art; the other leads to a new fiction,
and conceals the art of disclosure or confession. The withdrawal from one story leads through analysis to the discovery
of another, and virtue lies in their balance. Such an under-
taking sounds difficult and ambitious, and, in fact, Nemerov
tries manfully to protect himself from undue pretentions, to
remain unconscious of design (even retaining "errors" in the
text). He adopts the method of free-association for his analysis, "a technique," he writes, "of fiction, or poetry, or
magic, more than specifically of psychoanalysis, an exploration into the unknown, which yet shows a tendency to complete itself daily, tendency to form." He knows, in other
words, that he has chosen a form-making method, and that
the forms it creates tend to be false, to be Everyman rather than himself. And it is this knowledge or awareness
that is the chief vehicle of the book's redemption.

Nevertheless, the method of free-association is fruit-
ful. It can produce an aphorism like this: "The novel is
marriage; Poetry is infidelity." And it seems quite appropriate to the "unknown," both in its own crudeness and in
its relation to the paralysis of the adventuring writer. The
method is exploratory. To paraphrase one of Nemerov's

dream-motifs, he must descend into the labyrinth of his own
soul (his UCS) in order to liberate the integrity he needs.
What he finds there, however, is not a simple child, an
original innocence, but a fertile monster of art, the monster
he must recognize and accept as himself, if he is to liberate
anything.   The motif suggests that to record the fictive life
is to watch Theseus turn into the Minotaur.

The primary quality of Nemerov's journal is not,
however, a romantic vision of the artist as hero.   Not only
does he find it probable that "the beast does not exist, " he
also finds it clear that "character-analysis" is, as Freud
pointed out, an endless process.   The origins and goals of
thought, like the beginnings and endings of novels, have a
way of meeting and forming a circle.   And Nemerov has a
fully ironic appreciation of this fact.   One of the circumstances associated at the beginning of the book with his writing problem is his sexual "estrangement" from his wife, who
is well-advanced in pregnancy.   He closes his journal casu-
ally with the note that his wife has just given birth to their
son: Ariadne producing the thread to lead Theseus (fertile
monster) out of his fictive self and back into life.

The book reveals more than anything else an intelligent, good-humored, and very human consciousness.   Nemerov introduces no new myths, personal or otherwise, that
might claim his reader's allegiance; and he is even at his
worst or slickest where he tries to be more than usually
sensitive or fresh.   At his best, his fluency is a form of
lucidity.   The book testifies to an uncommon skill, an intelligence broad and flexible enough to be deftly ironic without
loss of sympathy.

13.   The Blue Swallows

a)   Reviewed by Joel Conarroe

Originally published as "Visions and Revisions,"
Shenandoah, Summer 1968.   Reprinted by permission of the author and Shenandoah.

Howard Nemerov, not an undergraduate hero, is one
of the makers who has managed, during the last twenty years,
to "alphabet the void" with a steady flow of poems, critical
essays, plays, and novels.   Implicit in all of his work has
been the assumption that art is vision, not dogma, and that
the poet, in re-deriving the possibilities of meaning from
matter, has as his principal goal the task of rendering the
highest kind of justice to the visible world.   An urbane, witty, elegant poet of considerable technical control, he is neither a thinker nor a spokesman for philosophers.   In fact,
when he does, on occasion, strive for Abstract Significance,
the poem tends to become brittle and thin, generally lacking
the naturalness and robust geniality that give the best of his
more typical work its appeal.   By "typical" I mean such poems as "The Town Dump," "Suburban Prophecy" and "Brainstorm" from Mirrors and Windows (1958), "The Scales of the
Eyes" sequence (justly celebrated by M. L. Rosenthal in The
New Poets) in New and Selected Poems (1960), and "A Spell
before Winter" and "Vermeer" from The Next Room of the
Dream (1962), to name only a non-anthologized few.   The
first lines of "Vermeer" provide a good description of his

137

own successful poems: "Taking what is, and seeing it as it is, / Pretending to no heroic stances or gestures, / Keeping it simple." In his new collection, The Blue Swallows, Mr. Nemerov only occasionally keeps it simple in the sense that he applies to Vermeer, but when he does the result is often quite wonderful.

The first of the book's four sections, "Legends," takes on "big" matters: life, death, creation, the fall, despair, art, hell of various sorts. Two of the section's finer poems, "To a Scholar in the Stacks" and "Lobsters" (fine in spite of "our needful food") are characteristic of the poet at his best in that each permits the poem's implications to radiate outward from a beautifully sustained image, keeping any symbolic meaning implicit in the situation. Another, a sort of Robert Frost narrative called "Learning by Doing," is symptomatic of a familiar Nemerov shortcoming, the tendency toward de trop. The first twenty-five lines describe the taking-down of a supposedly rotten tree, touch on the possibility of neighbors sawing up a man before he falls, and end with a moving line about the absent-minded blue raining in on us. One sits back, lets the poem happen, then discovers that there is more, eighteen lines more. (One learns to turn pages cautiously, hoping a pleasure just experienced will not be undercut by a generous excess.) It turns out that the wood was good after all, that the "experts," as always, are wrong, and that there is a moral: "You learn to bury your mistakes." The speaker justifies the bromidic conclusion by earlier belittling the bromides of others, the "they" who "say." (Nemerov often refers to "they," sometimes labelling them precisely--demographers, Treasury officials, Directors--but often letting them remain an unspecified enemy, strawmen unseen but heard who must

be put down because what they say is neither good nor true.)
To return to the tree, the ponderous conclusions, all inter-
estingly implicit in the opening description and elaboration,
blight the poem.   A little more than a little is by much too
much.

A similar lapse, found in the second section, is
called "The Night before Christmas."   The first half speaks
convincingly to any delinquent son or father who has ever
bought tacky gifts at Howard Johnson's on the way home:

> I am buying presents for everyone.
> It is very late, but better late,
> They say, than never.   I want
> Everyone to be happy, but admit
> I frequently do not do enough
> To implement this wish.   Now
> It is late, December Twenty-Fourth
> Darkens, and I, with others
> Scourged by the same conviction
> Of an absolute deliquency,
> Am walking the cold avenue
> Between the lines of brilliant windows
> Filled with impersonal satisfactions.
> I clutch my money, I shudder with cold,
> I go on attempting to buy
> The happiness of others.

Despite the too obvious final three lines, the section stands
as a simple but telling apercu.   This does not satisfy the
poet, however, and he goes on to make Statements about
crucifying Christ and buying Him cathedrals for Christmas,
spilling money in the dark river that ebbs, about the "price
of prices," and "the potlatch of time"--what oft, in short,
was thought, and oft as well expressed.

The second section, "The Great Society," contains
the overt satire we have come to expect (and welcome) in
Nemerov.   Unfortunately, his celebrated bookish comedy
sometimes works against him.   Anyone who eats regularly

in a faculty club knows that when wit becomes compulsive it
often induces a stupor made bearable only by the realization
that, like the soup du jour, it is transient.   Mr. Nemerov's
misses are recorded for the ages by the University of Chicago Press.   It is remarkable that a poet capable of the brilliant "Lot Later," "The Sparrow in the Zoo," and "Drama"
could commit, say, "the calorie count / of the Diet of
Worms," "Her bangles bangle," or the footnote description
of the Waldorf-Astoria in his Eliot spoof: "An hotel in New
York City." (This parody of The Waste Land, by the way,
completely misses the point of Eliot's own playfulness.)   The
following joke, "A Modern Poet," is from the new collection:

> Crossing at rush hour the Walt Whitman Bridge,
> He stopped at the Walt Whitman Shopping Center
> And bought a paperback copy of Leaves of Grass.
> Fame is the spur, he figured; given a Ford
> Foundation Fellowship, he'd buy a Ford.

One central problem with Mr. Nemerov's satire is that his
targets are often so thoroughly arrowed: Ike's prose "style,"
TV commercials, L-shaped ranch-type homes, committee
meetings, the supermarket, academic idiots.   "The Full
Professor" who manages to publish and perish is a case in
point.   This is a sad old joke, "discovered," surely, by
every graduate student since Moses.

The book's third and fourth section, "Figures" (twelve
lyrics, mostly in short lines) and "The Blue Swallows," contain, in addition to the moving title poem, several triumphs,
most notably "Celestial Globe," "The Beekeeper Speaks . . .
And Is Silent," and the superb "The Mud Turtle."   In the
latter poem, in which the reverberations are allowed to fall
where they may, the old turtle is called "A black planet,"
reminding us of this poet's happy penchant for eccentric epi-
thet.   Elsewhere in the collection a cherry tree full of birds

and squirrels is called "a minor universe," and a bee is
praised as "a totalitarian Don Juan." I should mention, while
on the subject of nature metaphors, that there is a moving
poem addressed to Robert Frost. There is also an implicit
tribute, in "Between the Window and the Screen," which describes an ant holding a dead fly's wing above his head, and
is thus a sort of ebony "Design."

Mr. Nemerov (like Frost) is conservative technically.
Theoretically he is often on the side of the ruffians, as his
critical essays show, but in practice he usually falls back on
conventional modes, suggesting that he prefers to defend new
growth with a pruning hook. The Blue Swallows contains a
variety of technical approaches, including heroic couplets,
short lined free verse, sonnets (rhymed and un-), modified
ottava rima, abab or abba stanzas, and others. It became
obvious several books ago, however, that his native language
is blank verse, and happily he never stays away from it for
long. (He also seems to work best in fifteen line segments.)
His line is supple, controlled, and solid, a wonderful instrument for his low keyed, conversational narratives and lyrics.
(I noticed in re-reading Endor that his stage directions even
sometimes fall, quite unintentionally, into exact iambic pentameter.) This is Mr. Nemerov's language. His other
forms sometimes sound translated, since any highly wrought
elaboration is at odds with his natural, unassuming under-
statement. His attempt at a sestina, for example ("Sarajevo") is a serious mistake, though I realize that in saying
so I may be charged with fulfilling the prophecy of one of the
"Gnomes"--"Father, he cried, after the critics' chewing, /
Forgive them, for they know not what I'm doing" (from The
Next Room of the Dream.)

b) Reviewed by Miller Williams

Almost all the "respectable" poetry currently coming
off the presses is boring; but it always has been, and the
good writers of bad poems are simply holding a solid front.
That only a small percentage of the poetry being published
now is exciting does nothing to distinguish our time from any
other, and is neither surprising nor discouraging. It is interesting, though, to see the way in which the dull is dull--
that is, how the poems keep the reader outside.

The majority of the poems contained in the books is-
sued this past quarter seem to have the same locks on them,
and they are fastened from the inside. They are over-intel-
lectual, pompous, almost without anything we can touch, subjective to the point of impenetrability, and rhetorically flat.
It is not an easy task to read through these scores of volumes of bloodless intrafraternity missiles, but it is made
more than worthwhile by the discovery of two or three books
here and there by poets of both skill and concern. Here are
the ones I found.

Howard Nemerov's The Blue Swallows . . . shows
the same fascination with the universe of Einstein that has
informed much of the poet's best work. He has carried on
the search for a kind of unified field theory, some metaphor
to bring time and space, being and non-being into harmony,
and to say where and what man is in the reality and illusion

of all this, and how the illusion is real.   This I think is
Nemerov at his best.

The opening poem, titled "The First Day," begins:

> Below the ten thousand billionth of a
>   centimeter
> Length ceases to exist.   Beyond three
>   billion light years
> The nebulae would have to exceed the
>   speed of light
> In order to be, which is impossible:
>   no universe.
> The long and short of it seems to be
>   that thought
> Can make itself unthinkable . . .

"When all analogies are broken," Nemerov says in
"The Black Museum," "the scene grows strange again.   At
last there is only one of everything."

Always man is there, hunting his way when "way"
may have no meaning he understands.   This is "The Human
Condition":

> In this motel where I was told to wait,
> The television screen is stood before
> The picture window.   Nothing could be
>   more
> Use to a man than knowing where
>   he's at.
> And I don't know, but pace the day
>   in doubt
> Between my looking in and looking out.

Nemerov is not always the metaphysician of time and
space; but when he is not speaking of man lost and overwhelmed within them, he is usually speaking of man lost
within the confusion of his own spirit and overwhelmed by
whatever it is that, as he wrote earlier in "Life Cycle of
Common Man," "makes the world his apple, and forces him
to eat."   His abiding concern is that of any sensible reader
in these days especially.

Which is not to say that the poems always work.   It
is true, as it has been true of Nemerov's earlier work, that
the puns and playfulness he is given to--and which are right
in the context a surprising percentage of the time--fall now
and then to flippancy and bad jokes.   Once in a while there
is too much of the professorial tone.   While the beginnings
and resolutions of almost all Nemerov's poems are as tight
as good craftsmanship can make them, a number have a curious way of going loose in rhythm and almost rambling in the
middle, so that the reader has the feeling of crossing a suspension bridge.   These are faults, if I read fairly; but they
are moved over without serious stumbling, and sometimes
are no more than the peculiar mark of the man.

The Blue Swallows is a book of serious poems loaded
with the kind of folly Nemerov makes himself the first brunt
of, and which the reader cannot quite escape.   Although now
and then funny, it is mostly dark and unsettling.

Part III:

HOWARD NEMEROV: A BIBLIOGRAPHY

by Bowie Duncan

This checklist attempts to make a preliminary compilation of all of Nemerov's works, their subsequent reprinting, and an annotated list of criticism of Mr. Nemerov. The early poetry and short stories are possibly not completely listed due to the number of little magazines Mr. Nemerov could have contributed to before he was accepted in more well-known and well-indexed periodicals. The essays should be more completely listed, as Furioso printed his early essays. The largest portion of the works about Mr. Nemerov are selected from book reviews, some of which were deleted because of their repetitiousness or lack of pertinent information. The only references which would be lacking and which should be included are those in books which I haven't seen. I welcome any additions and corrections.

Bowie Duncan

I. WORKS BY HOWARD NEMEROV

A. BOOKS

1. Books by Howard Nemerov

The Image and the Law.   New York: Henry Holt and Company, 1947.   Contents: 54 poems.
> The following poems appear in print for the first time: "From a Record of Disappointment," "The Truth of the Matter," "Two Poems," "Portrait of Three Conspirators," "The Place of Value," "Under the Bell Jar," "The Master at a Mediterranean Port," "Observations of October," "Metropolitan Sunday," "Warning: Children at Play," "Two Sides to an Outside," "A Morality," "Epitaph on a Philosopher," "The Baron Baedeker," "Crocodile at the Ancient Tombs," "Refusal of a Kindness Offered," "Autumnal," "For the Squadron," "For W--," "September Shooting," "According to His Seasons," "To the Memory of John Wheelwright," "Anniversary," "Lot's Wife," "An Old Photograph," "The Photograph of a Girl," "On Reading 'The Love and Death of Cornet Christopher Rilke,'" "Sestina II," "The Fortune Teller," "Advice from the Holy Tomb," "Unscientific Postscript."

The Melodramatists.   New York: Random House, 1949.
> Contents: a novel.

Guide to the Ruins.   New York: Random House, 1950.
> Contents: 41 poems.
> The following poems appear in print for the first time: "Guide to the Ruins," "On a Text," "Mars," "Peace in Our Time," "Song," "To a Friend," "Grand Central, with Soldiers," "The Hero Comes Home in His Hamper," "The Brief Journey West," "Succession," "Fragment from Correspondence," "Sonnet," "Still Life I," "Still Life II," "Still Life III," "Antigone," "Sonnet," "A Lean and Hungry Look."

Federigo, or the Power of Love.   Boston: Little,   Brown
   and Company, 1954.   Contents: a novel.

The Salt Garden.   Boston: Little,   Brown and Company,
   1955.   Contents: 35 poems.
   The following poems appear in print for the first time:
      "Zalamoxis," "Midsummer's Day," "The First Leaf,"
      "The Cuckoo King," "Dialectical Songs I-III," "Re-
      turned to Europe," "Instructions for Use of This Toy,"
      "An Issue of Life," "The Deposition," "The Market-
      place," "The Book of Kells," "Sleeping Beauty,"
      "Deep Woods."

The Homecoming Game.   New York: Simon and Schuster,
   1957.   Contents: a novel.

Mirrors and Windows.   Chicago: University of Chicago
   Press, 1958.   Contents: 51 poems.
   The following poems appear in print for the first time:
      "The Mirror," "The Sunglasses," "Distraction,"
      "False Solomon's Seal," "Suburban Prophecy," "IX
      Epigrams," "Reflections on the Seizure of the Suez,"
      "Seven Macabre Songs," "A Singular Metamorphosis,"
      "Drama," "Tale," "Moonshine," "Canossa," "Student
      Dies in 100 Yard Dash," "Limits," "Maia."

A Commodity of Dreams and Other Stories.   New York:
   Simon and Schuster, 1959.   Contents: 14 short stories.
   The following stories are printed for the first time:
      "The Guilty Shall Be Found Out and Punished," "A
      Commodity of Dreams," "The Ocean to Cynthia,"
      "Visiting the Sick," "The Sorcerer's Eye."

New and Selected Poems.   Chicago: University of Chicago
   Press, 1960.   Contents: 58 poems.
   The following poems are printed for the first time:
      "To H. M.," "The Sparrow in the Zoo."
   Section I contains poems from periodicals, section II con-
      tains selections from Mirrors and Windows and The
      Salt Garden, and Section III selects from Guide to the
      Ruins and The Image and the Law.

The Next Room of the Dream.   Chicago: University of Chicago Press, 1962.   Contents: 51 poems and two plays.
   The following appear for the first time:
      "To Clio, Muse of History," "Goldfish," "Fontenelle,"
      "Don Juan to the Statue," "Somewhere," "Polonius

        Passing Through a Stage," "The View from Pisgah,"
        "Metamorphosis," "Lion & Honeycomb," "The Fall A-
        gain," "Vaudeville & Critique," "To the Bleeding Hearts
        Association of American Novelists," "The Poet at
        Forty."

Endor. Nashville: Abingdon Press, 1962. Contents: a
  play.

Poetry and Fiction: Essays. New Brunswick, New Jersey:
  Rutgers University Press, 1963. Contents: 55 essays.
        The following essay appears in print for the first time:
        "Calculation Raised to Mystery."

Journal of the Fictive Life. New Brunswick: University of
  Rutgers Press, 1965. Contents: a journal dealing with
        Nemerov's attempt to rid himself of a writing block.

The Blue Swallows. Chicago: University of Chicago Press,
  1967. Contents: 67 poems.
        The following poems appear in print for the first time:
        "The First Day," "Creation of Anguish," "Learning by
        Doing," "In the Commercial Gardens," "The Cherry
        Tree," "A Life," "Epitaph," "An Old Colonial Imperi-
        alist," "Beyond the Pleasure Principle," "Departure of
        the Ships," "The Night Before Christmas," "Sunday,"
        "A Way of Life," "Money," "Make Love Not War,"
        "To the Governor & Legislature of Massachusetts,"
        "A Full Professor," "Grace To Be Said Before Com-
        mittee Meetings," "A Modern Poet," "On the Plat-
        form," "The Great Society, Mark X," "The Dream of
        Flying Comes of Age," "Grace To Be Said at the Su-
        permarket," "August, 1945," "The Flame of a Candle,"
        "Between the Window and the Screen," "Decorated Skull
        in a University Museum," "Dead River," "In the Black
        Museum," "The Race," "Sightseers," "Thought,"
        "Style," "Celestial Globe," "One Way," "The Blue
        Swallows," "The Beekeeper Speaks . . . And Is Silent,"
        "Firelight in Sunlight."

A Sequence of Seven With a Drawing by Ron Slaughter.
  Detroit: The Tinker Press, 1967. Contents: 7 poems.
        From the acknowledgement: "These poems are drawn
        from a new collection, The Blue Swallows. . . ."
        The seven poems are: "The Flame of a Candle,"
        "Decorated Skull in a University Museum," "Between
        the Window and the Screen," "Thought," "In the Black

Museum," "Dead River," "Celestial Globe."

Winter Lightning. London: Rapp and Whiting, 1968. Contents: 41 poems collected chronologically from his books
from The Salt Garden to The Blue Swallows.

The Painter Dreaming in the Scholar's House. New York:
The Phoenix Book Shop, 1968. Contents: a poem.
From the acknowledgement: "26 copies lettered A to Z."

2. Books edited by Howard Nemerov

Henry Wadsworth Longfellow, Selected Poems. New York:
Dell Books, 1965. Contents: besides the poems, an essay by Nemerov: "On Longfellow."

Moore, Marianne. Poetry and Criticism. Cambridge, Massachusetts: Adams House and Lowell House Printers,
1965. Contents: Marianne Moore's response to four questions about poetry.

Poets on Poetry. New York: Basic Books, 1966. Contents:
a collection of contemporary poets' responses to four
questions about poetry, with Nemerov also offering his
own response.

3. Contributions to Books

[untitled comment about his favorite poem, "Runes,"] Poets
Choice, Paul Engle and Joseph Lang, eds. New York:
Dial Press, 1962. Pp. 186-187.

[untitled introduction to the book] Poetic Diction, Owen Bar-
field, New York: McGraw-Hill and Company, 1964.
Pp. 1-9.

"The Two Gentlemen of Verona: A Commentary," The Two
Gentlemen of Verona, William Shakespeare, Richard Wilbur, ed. New York: Dell Books, 1964. Pp. 1-10.

"Composition and Fate in the Short Novel," Perspectives in
Contemporary Criticism, Sheldon Norman Grebstein, ed.
New York: Harper and Roe, 1968. Pp. 120-132.

4. Broadsides

"Small Moment" San Francisco: Poems in Folio, 1957.
   Contents: a poem.
   Acknowledgement reads: "This poem was printed at the
      Ward Richie Press in Los Angeles from Bembo types
      in an edition of 1150 copies of which 150 are on Maid-
      stone hand-made paper and signed by the author."

"Storm Windows" Detroit, 1965.   Contents: a poem.
   Acknowledgement reads: "Seventy-seven copies reprinted
      in MCLXV by Wish."

"Dangers of Reasoning by Analogy" Rochester, Michigan,
   1966.   Contents: a poem.
   Acknowledgement reads: "Eighty copies are here first
      printed by Walter S. Hamody on the Washington in
      Robert Runsen's shop near Rochester, Michigan."

B. PERIODICALS

1. Poetry

"Inventory and Statement: a Declaration," Harvard Advocate,
   (March, 1940), 16.

"Poem," Harvard Advocate, (March, 1941), 10.

"Notes on a New England Winter," Kenyon Review, II
   (Autumn, 1941), 408.

"To the Memory of John Wheelwright," Vice Versa, I (January, 1942), 20-21.

"On the Flight into Egypt," Vice Versa, I (January, 1942),
   21-22.

"No More of Sanctity," Decision, III (February, 1942), 23.

"Sigmund Freud," Poetry, LXII (August, 1943), 261.

"In the Glass of Fashion," Briarcliff Quarterly, II (April,
   1946), 35.   Collected in The Image and the Law.

"The Soldier Who Lived Through the War," Saturday Review
of Literature, XXIX (March 23, 1946), 48. Collected in
The Image and the Law.

"Frozen City," Sewanee Review, LIV (October, 1946), 660.
Collected in The Image and the Law.
Reprinted: Fifteen Modern American Poets, George P.
Elliott, ed. New York: Holt, Rinehart and Winston,
1959. P. 103.

"The Stare of the Man from the Provinces," Furioso, II
(Fall, 1946), 50. Collected in The Image and the Law
and Selected Poems.

"Who Did Not Die in Vain," Furioso, II (Fall, 1946), 52.
Collected in The Image and the Law.

"Europe," Furioso, II (Fall, 1946), 51. Collected in The
Image and the Law.

"The Triumph of Education," New Yorker, XXII (December
26, 1946), 60. Collected in The Image and the Law.

"Poem of A Death," Furioso, II (Summer, 1947), 35. The
poem was published under the pseudonym of S. J. Can-
brode.

"Frescoes For the Moscow Subway," Furioso II (Summer,
1947), 62. Collected in Guide to the Ruins and New
and Selected Poems.

"Various Vacations, Vacancies," Touchstone, I (November,
1947), 32.

"Full Small Ballad," Touchstone, I (November, 1947), 33.

"Last Letter, with Snapshots," Touchstone, I (December,
1947), 9.

"Landscape in America," Furioso, III (Winter, 1947), 45.

"Carol," Hudson Review, I (Summer, 1948), 204. Collected
in Guide to the Ruins and New and Selected Poems.

"The Bacterial War," Hudson Review, I (Summer, 1948),
204. Collected in Guide to the Ruins.

"Four Sonnets," Furioso, III (Fall, 1948), 16.   Collected
   in Guide to the Ruins.

"The Old Country," Furioso, III (Autumn, 1948), 12.   Collected in Guide to the Ruins.

"Trial & Death, a Double Feature," Furioso, III (Autumn,
   1948), 12.   Collected in Guide to the Ruins.

"Sonnet at Easter," Furioso, III (Autumn, 1948), 14.   Collected in Guide to the Ruins.
      Reprinted: Fifteen Modern American Poets.   George P.
         Elliott, ed. New York: Holt, Rinehart and Winston,
         1959. P. 109.

"Elegy of Last Resort," Sewanee Review, LVI (October,
   1948), 654.   Collected in Guide to the Ruins.

"Virgin & Martyr," Furioso, IV (Summer, 1949), 35.   Collected in Guide to the Ruins.

"A Fable of the War," Furioso, IV (Summer, 1949), 36.
   Collected in Guide to the Ruins.
      Reprinted: New Poets of England and America.   Donald
         Hall and Robert Pack, eds. New York: Meridian
         Books, 1957. P. 250.
      Five American Poets, Thom Gunn and Ted Hughes, eds.
         London: Faber and Faber, 1963. P. 51.

"To the Babalonians," Furioso, IV (Summer, 1949), 37.
   Collected in Guide to the Ruins.

"A Poem of Margery Kemp," Hudson Review, II (Summer,
   1949), 240.   Collected in Guide to the Ruins.
      Reprinted: Fifteen Modern American Poets, George P.
         Elliott, ed. New York: Meridian, 1959. P. 108.

"A Song of Degrees," Commentary, VII (Summer, 1949), 283.
   Collected in Guide to the Ruins.

"Madrigal," Hudson Review, II (Summer, 1949), 240.   Collected in Guide to the Ruins.

"The Earthquake in the West," Furioso, IV (Autumn, 1949),
   22.   Collected in Guide to the Ruins.

"To A Friend Gone to Fight for the Kuomingtang," Partisan

Review, XVI (December, 1949), 1220.

"The Second-Best Bed," Furioso, IV (Autumn, 1949), 21.
Collected in Guide to the Ruins and New and Selected
Poems.

"Sunday at the End of Summer," New Yorker, XXVI (September 30, 1950), 82.   Collected in The Salt Garden and
New and Selected Poems.

"The End Crowning the Work," New Yorker, XXVI (December 2, 1950), 84.

"Nicodemus," Commentary, IX (Winter, 1950), 56.   Collected in Guide to the Ruins.

"Reflection," Furioso, VI (Spring, 1951), 58.

"A Harvest Home," Furioso, VI (Spring, 1951), 58.   Collected in The Salt Garden.

"Moralities," Poetry, LXXX (July 1, 1951), 199.

"Sonnet," Furioso, VI (Spring, 1951), 58.

"The Salt Garden," Western Review, XVI (Autumn, 1951), 19.
Collected in The Salt Garden.
Reprinted: New Poets of England and America, Donald
     Hall and Robert Pack, eds.   New York: Meridian
     Books, 1957, P. 245.
     Fifteen Modern American Poets, George P. Elliott, ed.
     New York: Holt, Rinehart and Winston, 1959.
     P. 118.
     Five American Poets,   Thom Gunn and Ted Hughes,
     eds.   London: Faber and Faber, 1963.   P. 52.

"The Scales of the Eyes, A Poem in the Form of a Text and
Variations," Sewanee Review, LX (January, 1952), 107-
116.   Collected in The Salt Garden and New and Selected
Poems.

"Gyroscope Top," New Yorker, XXVII (April 19, 1952), 120.

"Dialogue," New Yorker, XXVIII (May 10, 1952), 116.   Collected in The Salt Garden.
Reprinted: Poetry for Pleasure, Hallmark Cards, eds.
     New York: Doubleday, 1960.   P. 80.

"Armistice," Gambit, I (Summer, 1952), 5.   Collected in
The Salt Garden.

"I Only Am Escaped Alone to Tell Thee," Hudson Review, V
(Autumn, 1952), 357.   Collected in The Salt Garden, New
and Selected Poems and The Winter Lightning.
   Reprinted: New Pocket Anthology of American Verse
      From Colonial Days to the Present, Oscar Williams,
         ed. New York: Pocket Books, 1955. P. 391.
   Five American Poets, Thom Gunn and Ted Hughes, eds.
      London: Faber and Faber, 1963. P. 39.

"Truth," Hudson Review, V (Autumn, 1952), 357.   Collected
in The Salt Garden, New and Selected Poems, and The
Winter Lightning.
   Reprinted: Modern Verse in English, 1900-1950, Allen
      Tate, ed. New York: Macmillan and Company, 1958.
         P. 628.

"Fall Song," Hudson Review, V (Autumn, 1952), 375.   Collected in The Salt Garden.

"The Gulls," Hudson Review, V (Autumn, 1952), 375.   Collected in The Salt Garden.

"The Sanctuary," Sewanee Review, LXI (October, 1953), 628.
Collected in The Salt Garden and New and Selected Poems.
   Reprinted: New Poets of England and America, Donald
      Hall and Robert Pack, eds. New York: Meridian
         Books, 1957. P. 249.
   Five American Poets, Thom Gunn and Ted Hughes, eds.
      London: Faber and Faber, 1963. P. 42.

"An Old War Plane," Sewanee Review, LXI (October, 1953),
629.   Collected in Mirrors and Windows.

"The Priest's Curse on Dancing," Atlantic Monthly, CXCII
(April, 1954), 44.   Collected in The Salt Garden.

"The Pond," New Yorker, XXX (September 4, 1954), 30.
Collected in The Salt Garden, New and Selected Poems
and The Winter Lightning.
   Reprinted: Fifteen Modern American Poets, George P.
      Elliott, ed. New York: Holt, Rinehart and Winston,
         1959. P. 114.

"The Old Soldiers' Home," Atlantic Monthly, CXCIV (September, 1955), 62. Collected in Mirrors and Windows.

"An Old Picture," Atlantic Monthly, CXCIV (December, 1954),
54. Collected in The Salt Garden.

"Sunderland," Poetry, LXXXVII (October, 1955), 35. Collected in Mirrors and Windows.

"Forecast," New Yorker, XXXI (February 1, 1956), 38.

"Lore," Nation, CLXXXII (April 14, 1956), 318. Collected
in Mirrors and Windows.

"Shells," Nation, CLXXXII (May 19, 1956), 437. Collected
in Mirrors and Windows and New and Selected Poems.

"Art Song," Poetry, LXXXVIII (Spring, 1956), 388. Collected
in Mirrors and Windows.

"The Loon's Cry," Sewanee Review, LXIV (Spring, 1956),
238.

"Ahasuerus," Accent, XVI (Spring, 1956), 89.

"The Fourth of July," Nation, CLXXXII (June 30, 1956), 553.

"Cloud Seeding," Poetry, LXXXVIII (Spring, 1956), 382.

"A Clock with No Hands," Poetry, LXXXVIII (Spring, 1956),
383.

"Political Reflection," Poetry, LXXXVIII (Spring, 1956),
387.
    Reprinted: Eight Lines Under, William Cole, ed. New
    York: Macmillan and Company, 1967. P. 104.

"The Wheel King," Poetry, LXXXVIII (Spring, 1956), 387.

"A Speckled Stone Mirror," Poetry, LXXXVIII (Spring,
1956), 384.

"The Battenkill in Winter," Poetry, LXXXVIII (Spring, 1956),
385.

"A Mobile of Carved Wooden Fish," Poetry, LXXXVIII
(Spring, 1956), 386.

"Sandpipers," New Yorker, XXII (August 4, 1956), 22.

"The Statues in the Public Gardens," Nation, CLXXXIII
   (August 25, 1956), 163.   Collected in Mirrors and Windows
   and New and Selected Poems.

"Reactionary History," Nation, CLXXXIII (November 10, 1956),
   414.

"Storm Windows," Nation, CLXXXIII (December 22, 1956),
   545.   Collected in Mirrors and Windows, New and Selected Poems, and The Winter Lightning.
   Reprinted: Poetry in English, Warren Taylor and Donald
      Hall, eds. New York: Macmillan and Company, 1963.
      P. 638.

"Endgeeste," Hika, (Winter, 1956), 17.   Collected in Mirrors and Windows.

"Absent-Minded Professor," Nation, CLXXXIV (March 9,
   1957), 222.   Collected in New and Selected Poems.
   Reprinted: Eight Lines and Under, William Cole, ed.
   New York: Macmillan and Company, 1967. P. 127.

"Witch of Endor," Nation, CLXXXIV (March 23, 1957), 258.

"Trees," Beloit Poetry Chapbook, No. V (Summer, 1957),
   38.   Collected in Mirrors and Windows, New and Selected Poems, and The Winter Lightning.
   Reprinted: Five American Poets, Thom Gunn and Ted
      Hughes, eds. London: Faber and Faber, 1963. P. 36.
      Art and Craft in Poetry, James Lape, ed.   New York:
      Ginn and Company, 1967.   P. 68.

"A Primer of the Daily Round," New Yorker, XXXIII (October 12, 1957), 46.   Collected in Mirrors and Windows
   and New and Selected Poems.

"The Map Maker on His Art," New Yorker, XXXIII (November 30, 1957), 54.   Collected in Mirrors and Windows.

"Town Dump, Wellfleet," Partisan Review, XXIV (Fall, 1957),
   582.   Collected in Mirrors and Windows and New and Selected Poems.

"The Dancer's Reply," Poetry, XCI (November, 1957), 77.

"Sarabande," Poetry, XCI (November, 1957), 78.   Collected
   in Mirrors and Windows and New and Selected Poems.

"Painting a Mountain Stream," Poetry, XCI (November,
   1957), 78.   Collected in Mirrors and Windows and New
   and Selected Poems.
   Reprinted: Five American Poets, Thom Gunn and Ted
      Hughes, eds.   London: Faber and Faber, 1963. P. 41.

"Holding the Mirror Up to Nature," Poetry, XCI (November,
   1957), 75.   Collected in Mirrors and Windows, New and
   Selected Poems and The Winter Lightning.
   Reprinted: Five American Poets, Thom Gunn and Ted
      Hughes, eds.   London: Faber and Faber, 1963. P. 41.

"A Day on the Big Branch," Poetry XCI (November, 1957),
   71.   Collected in Mirrors and Windows, New and Selected Poems and The Winter Lightning.

"Brainstorm," Quarterly Review of Literature, IX (Winter,
   1957), 29.   Collected in Mirrors and Windows, New and
   Selected Poems, and The Winter Lightning.
   Reprinted: Five American Poets, Thom Gunn and Ted
      Hughes, eds.   London: Faber and Faber, 1963. P. 50.
      Today's Poets, Chad Walsh, ed.   New York: Charles
         Scribners and Sons, 1964.   P. 256.

"Lightning Storm on Fuji," Quarterly Review of Literature,
   IX (Winter, 1957), 30.   Collected in Mirrors and Windows.

"Orphic Scenario," Quarterly Review of Literature, IX
   (Winter, 1957), 32.   Collected in Mirrors and Windows.

"Moses," Quarterly Review of Literature, IX (Winter, 1957),
   25.   Collected in Mirrors and Windows.

"Writing," New Yorker, XXXIII (December 14, 1957), 46.
   Collected in Mirrors and Windows.
   Reprinted: Five American Poets, Thom Gunn and Ted
      Hughes, eds.   London: Faber and Faber, 1963. P. 40.
      The Force of Few Words, Jacob Korg, ed.   New York:
         Holt, Rinehart and Winston, 1966.   P. 390.

"The Murder of William Remington," Nation, CLXXXV (December 28, 1957), 448.   Collected in Mirrors and Windows
   and New and Selected Poems.
   Reprinted: Five American Poets, Thom Gunn and Ted

Hughes, eds.   London: Faber and Faber, 1963.
P. 44.

"To Lu Chi," Accent, XVII (Winter, 1957), 16.   Collected
in Mirrors and Windows, New and Selected Poems, and
Winter Lightning.

"Boom," Nation, CLXXXVI (January 25, 1958), 81.   Collected
in New and Selected Poems.
    Reprinted: The Modern Poets, John Malcolm Brinnin and
    Bill Read, eds.   New York: McGraw-Hill, 1963.
    P. 252.
    Poems of Doubt and Belief, Tom Driver and Robert
        Pack, eds.   New York: Macmillan and Company,
    1964. P. 169.
    The American Experience: Poetry, Dora V. Smith,
        ed. New York: Macmillan and Company, 1968.
    Pp. 344-346.

"To Certain Wits," Silo, (May, 1958), 5.

"The Ice House in Summer," Partisan Review, XXV (Summer, 1958), 369.   Collected in New and Selected Poems.

"A Picture," Nation, CLXXXVII (September 20, 1958), 157.
Collected in The Next Room of the Dream.

"On Certain Wits," Nation, CLXXXVII (September 6, 1958),
119.

"To David, About His Education," Nation, CLXXXVII (October 4, 1958), 195. Collected in The Next Room of the
Dream.
    Reprinted: Art and Craft in Poetry, James Lape, ed.
    New York: Ginn and Company, 1967.   P. 510.

"Home for the Holidays," Virginia Quarterly Review,
XXXIV (Winter, 1958), 55.   Collected in Mirrors and
Windows.

"The Junction: A Warm Afternoon," New Yorker, XXXV
(May 16, 1959), 39.   Collected in The Next Room of the
Dream.

"Runes," Poetry, XCIII (Summer, 1959), 281.   Collected in
New and Selected Poems and The Winter Lightning.

Reprinted: Poets Choice, Paul Engle and Joseph Lang-
land, eds. New York: Dial Press, 1962. Pp. 178-186.
Five American Poets, Thom Gunn and Ted Hughes, eds.
London: Faber and Faber, 1963. P. 46 ["Runes
VIII"]
Today's Poets, Chad Walsh, ed. New York: Charles
Scribners, 1964. P. 257. ["Runes VII"]
Art and Craft in Poetry, James Lape, ed. New York:
Ginn and Company, 1967. Pp. 248, 381. ["Runes
III, VIII"]

"Going Away," American Scholar, XXVIII (Summer, 1959),
308. Collected in New and Selected Poems.

"Death and the Maiden," Poetry, XCIV (Summer, 1959), 396.
Collected in New and Selected Poems and The Winter
Lightning.
Reprinted: Five American Poets, Thom Gunn and Ted
Hughes, eds. London: Faber and Faber, 1963.
P. 47.

"The Remorse for Time," Audience, VI (Autumn, 1959), 86.
Collected in New and Selected Poems.

"Burning the Leaves," [London] Times Literary Supplement,
3010 (November 6, 1959) Supplement to the Supplement
xvii. Collected in The Next Room of the Dream.

"Elegy for a Nature Poet," New Yorker, XXXV (December
12, 1959), 50. Collected in The Next Room of the Dream.
Reprinted: Poems on Poetry, Robert Wallace, ed. New
York: E. P. Dutton, 1965. P. 54.
Poetry: An Introduction, William Lane, ed. New
York: D. C. Heath, 1968. P. 32.

"Debate with the Rabbi," Nation, CXC (February 13, 1960),
152. Collected in The Next Room of the Dream.
Reprinted: Poetry for Pleasure. New York: Doubleday
1960. P. 353.

"Life Cycle of a Common Man," Noble Savage, I (1960), 206.
Collected in New and Selected Poems.
Reprinted: Five American Poets, Thom Gunn and Ted
Hughes, eds. London: Faber and Faber, 1963. P. 45.

"Tragedy in Garden City," Nation, CXC (April 23, 1960),
365.

"Blue Suburban," New Yorker, XXXVI (July 2, 1960), 162.
    Collected in The Next Room of the Dream.

"Moment," New Yorker, XXXVI (August 20, 1960), 27. Col-
    lected in New and Selected Poems.
    Reprinted: Poems of Doubt and Belief, Tom Driver and
        Robert Pack, eds. New York: Macmillan and Com-
        pany, 1964. P. 169.

"At a Country Hotel," Nation, CXCI (September 10, 1960),
    134.   Collected in The Winter Lightning and The Next
    Room of the Dream.
    Reprinted: Poems to Read About, Edward Hodnett, ed.
    New York: W. W. Norton Company, 1968. P. 253.

"Angel and Stone," New Yorker, XXVI (September 3, 1960),
    30.   Collected in New and Selected Poems and The Winter
    Lightning.

"Politics," Nation, CXCI (October 29, 1960), 336.

"The View from an Attic Window," Colorado Quarterly, IX
    (Autumn, 1960), 163.   Collected in New and Selected
    Poems and The Winter Lightning.

"Maestria," Carleton Miscellany, I (Winter, 1960), 32.
    Collected in New and Selected Poems.

"Realities," Choice, I (Spring, 1961), 19.   Collected in The
    Next Room of the Dream.

"A Predecessor of Perseus," Carleton Miscellany, II (Spring,
    1961), 22.   Collected in The Next Room of the Dream.

"Make Big Money at Home! Write Poems in Spare Time,"
    Carleton Miscellany, II (Spring, 1961), 23.   Collected in
    The Next Room of the Dream.

"Gnomes," Carleton Miscellany, II (Spring, 1961), 24.   Col-
    lected in The Next Room of the Dream.

"Maiden with Orb and Planets," Hudson Review, XIV (Sum-
    mer, 1961), 216.   Collected in The Next Room of the
    Dream.

"The First Point of Aries," Hudson Review, XIV (Summer,
    1961), 216.   Collected in The Next Room of the Dream.

"Lot Later," Carleton Miscellany, II (Fall, 1961), 36. Collected in The Next Room of the Dream.

"The Daily Globe," Harpers, CCXXIII (November, 1961), 39. Collected in The Next Room of the Dream.

"The Private Eye," Poetry, XCIX (November, 1961), 84. Collected in The Next Room of the Dream.

"The Dragonfly," Poetry, XCIX (November, 1961), 83. Collected in The Next Room of the Dream.

"To the Mannequins," Poetry, XCIX (November, 1961), 82. Collected in The Next Room of the Dream.

"The End of Summer School," Poetry, XCIX (November, 1961), 81. Collected in The Next Room of the Dream.

"On the Threshold of His Greatness, the Poet Comes Down with a Sore Throat," New Yorker, XXXVII (November 25, 1961), 60. Collected in The Next Room of the Dream.

"Nothing Will Yield," Noble Savage, III (1961), 123. Collected in The Next Room of the Dream.

"Cybernetics," Carleton Miscellany, III (Winter, 1962), 3. Collected in The Blue Swallows.

"Journey of the Snowmen," New Yorker, XXXVI (January 13, 1962), 81. Collected in The Next Room of the Dream.

"Winter Exercise," Saturday Evening Post, CCXXXV (February 3, 1962), 30. Collected in The Next Room of the Dream.

"Human Things," New Yorker, XXXVII (February 17, 1962), 30. Collected in The Next Room of the Dream and The Winter Lightning.
   Reprinted: Today's Poets, Chad Walsh, ed. New York: Charles Scribners, 1964. P. 265.
   Studying Poetry, Karl Kroeber and John Lyons, eds. New York: Harper and Row, 1965. P. 222.

"The Ground Swayed," Silo, (Spring, 1962), Insert.

"One Forever Alien," Reporter, XXVI (March 29, 1962), 40.

"These Words Also," Poetry, C (June, 1962), 144. Collected in The Next Room of the Dream and The Winter Lightning.

"Promethus at Radio City," Poetry, C (June, 1962), 143.

"Vermeer," Poetry, C (June, 1962), 142. Collected in The Next Room of the Dream.

"The Iron Characters," Outsider, #2 (Summer, 1962), 13. Collected in The Next Room of the Dream.

"De Anima," Poetry, C (June, 1962), 141. Collected in The Next Room of the Dream and The Winter Lightning. Reprinted: Today's Poets, Chad Walsh, ed. New York: Charles Scribners, 1964. P. 265.

"Idea," Poetry, CI (October, 1962), 84.

"An Interview," Carleton Miscellany, III (Fall, 1962), 7.

"From the Desk of the Lauriate: For Immediate Release," Carleton Miscellany, III (Fall, 1962), 8.

"Lobsters," Reporter, XXVII (November 8, 1962), 48. Collected in The Blue Swallows.

"The Dial Tone," New Yorker, XXXVIII (November 24, 1962), 50. Collected in The Next Room of the Dream. Reprinted: Today's Poets, Chad Walsh, ed. New York: Charles Scribners, 1964. P. 266.

"A Spell Before Winter," New Yorker, XXXVIII (November 3, 1962), 52. Collected in The Next Room of the Dream and The Winter Lightning. Reprinted: Today's Poets, Chad Walsh, ed. New York: Charles Scribners, 1964. P. 265.

"Santa Claus," Reporter, XXVII (December 20, 1962), 44. Collected in The Next Room of the Dream. Reprinted: The American Experience: Poetry, Dora V. Smith, ed. New York: Macmillan and Company, 1968. P. 347.

"Sight Seers," Approach, #47 (Spring, 1963), 2. Collected in The Blue Swallows and The Winter Lightning.

"Landscape with Figures," Nation, CXCVI (April 27, 1963),

346.   Collected in The Blue Swallows and The Winter
Lightning.

"The Breaking of Rainbows," Reporter, XXVIII (May 23,
1963), 49.   Collected in The Blue Swallows and The
Winter Lightning.

"The Sweeper of Ways," Shenandoah, XII (Spring, 1963), 11.
Collected in The Blue Swallows and The Winter Lightning.

"Nobody Ever Said," Shenandoah, XII (Spring, 1963), 10.

"The Distances They Keep," Shenandoah, XII (Spring, 1963),
12.   Collected in The Blue Swallows.

"Two Girls," Shenandoah, XII (Spring, 1963), 9.   Collected
in The Blue Swallows.

"Sarajevo," Reporter, XXIX (July 18, 1963), 51.   Collected
in The Blue Swallows and The Winter Lightning.

"The Human Condition," Kenyon Review, XXVI (Winter, 1964),
232.   Collected in The Blue Swallows and The Winter
Lightning.

"Growing a Ghost," Hollins Critic, I (April, 1964), 9.   Collected in The Blue Swallows.

"The May Day Dancing," New Yorker, XXXX (May 2, 1964),
48.   Collected in The Blue Swallows and The Winter
Lightning.

"The Mud Turtle," New Yorker, XXXX (July 25, 1964), 32.
Collected in The Blue Swallows and The Winter Lightning.

"Learning By Doing," Kenyon Review, XXVI (Summer, 1964),
387.

"For Robert Frost, in the Autumn After His Death," Kenyon
Review, XXVI (Summer, 1964), 388.   Collected in The
Blue Swallows.

"Interiors," Kenyon Review, XXVI (Summer, 1964), 513.
Collected in The Blue Swallows and The Winter Lightning.

"Summer's Elegy," Kenyon Review, XXVI (Summer, 1964),
512.   Collected in The Blue Swallows.

"A Negro Cemetery Next to a White One," The Message, (Summer, 1964), 22.   Collected in The Blue Swallows.

"Metamorphoses," [London] Stand, VI (Fall, 1964), 67.

"Small Moment," Yale Literary Magazine, CXXXIII (April, 1965), 48.   Collected in The Blue Swallows.

"The Companions," New Yorker, XLI (August 21, 1965), 30. Collected in The Blue Swallows and The Winter Lightning.

"A Relation of Art and Life," Reporter, XXXIII (September 23, 1965), 54.   Collected in The Blue Swallows and The Winter Lightning.

"Interiors," [London] Agenda, IV (Summer, 1966), 19.

"At the Airport," New Yorker, XLII (November 12, 1966), 66.   Collected in The Blue Swallows.

"Christmas Morning," Folio, IV (Fall, 1965), 3.   Collected in The Blue Swallows.

"Enthusiasm for Hats," Vassar Review, XVIII (Winter, 1966), 5.   Collected in The Blue Swallows.

"Keeping Informed in D. C." Polemic, XI (Winter, 1966), 51. Collected in The Blue Swallows.

"Dangers of Reasoning by Analogy," Polemic, XI (Winter, 1966), 41.

"This, That and the Other," Silo, (Spring, 1966), 17.   Collected in The Blue Swallows.

"The View," New Yorker, XLII (October 29, 1966), 64.   Collected in The Blue Swallows and The Winter Lightning.

"Marriage of Heaven and Earth," New Yorker, XLII (December 10, 1966), 146.

"To A Scholar in the Stacks," American Scholar, XXXVI (Spring, 1967), 218.   Collected in The Blue Swallows.

"An Old Colonial," Tri-Quarterly, VIII (Winter, 1967), 110.

"TV," Tri-Quarterly, VIII (Winter, 1967), 156.

"The Cherry Tree," Tri Quarterly, VIII (Winter, 1967), 124.
Collected in The Blue Swallows.

"A Full Professor," Tri-Quarterly, VIII (Winter, 1967), 132.
Collected in The Blue Swallows.

"Projection," Atlantic Monthly, CCXIX (May, 1967), 87.
Collected in The Blue Swallows.

"Presidential Address to a Party of Exiles Leaving for the
Moon," New Yorker, XLIII (August 12, 1967), 92. Collected in The Blue Swallows.

"The Rope's End," Atlantic Monthly, CCXX (September,
1967), 103.

"Retirement on the Subjunctive Plan," Harvard Advocate,
CIII (Spring, 1969), 15.

"Late Butterflies," New Yorker, XLV (October, 1969), 38.

"On Being Asked for a Peace Poem," Saturday Review,
LIII (March 28, 1970), 74.

"The Most Expensive Picture in the World," New Republic,
CLXII (March 28, 1970), 17.

"Brueghel: The Triumph of Time," New Yorker, XLVI
(April 18, 1970), 48.

"One Moment in Eternity," New Republic, CLXII (May 30,
1970), 25.

"September, The First Day of School," New Yorker, XLVI,
(September 19, 1970), 42.

"Myth and Ritual," New Republic, CLXIII (November 21,
1970), 21.

"Two Views of a Philosopher," Shenandoah, XXI (September,
1970), 56.

2.   Short Stories

"Justa Little Smile," Harvard Advocate, (April, 1940), 17.

"Gerhart Otto," Harvard Advocate, (September, 1941), 17.

"The Native in the World," Harvard Advocate, (July, 1941),
7.

"Exchange of Men," Story, XXIX (November, 1946), 9-17.
(Written with W. R. Johnson under the pseudonym, "J.
Cross").
Reprinted: Stories of Sudden Truth, J. I. Green, ed.
New York: Ballentine, 1953. Pp. 190-202.
The Modern Short Story in the Making, Whit and Hallie
Burnett, eds. New York: Hawthorne Books, 1964.
Pp. 292-302.
Fiction of the Forties, Whit Burnett, ed. New York:
Dutton Press, 1949. Pp. 589-602.

"The Amateurs," Furioso, II (Summer, 1947), 37-54. Col-
lected in Commodity of Dreams and Other Stories.
Reprinted: New Directions in Prose and Poetry, James
Laughlin, ed. New Jersey: Blue Ridge Mountain
Press, 1948. Pp. 220-235.

"The Web of Life," Furioso, III, (Autumn, 1948), 28. Collected in A Commodity of Dreams and Other Stories.

"The Twitch," Gambit, I (Spring, 1952), 5. Collected in
A Commodity of Dreams and Other Stories.
Reprinted: The Chosen, H. U. Ribalow, ed. London:
Abelard Schuman, 1959. Pp. 226-236.

"Yore," Hudson Review, VI (Winter, 1954), 550-559. Collected in A Commodity of Dreams and Other Stories.
Reprinted: Best American Short Stories, 1955, David
Burnett, ed. Boston: Houghton, Mifflin Company,
1955. Pp. 231-241.

"Tradition," Kenyon Review, XVII (Summer, 1955), 408-424.
Collected in A Commodity of Dreams and Other Stories.
Reprinted: Prize Stories O'Henry Awards, Paul Engle
and Hansford Martin, eds. New York: Doubleday,
1955. Pp. 114-128.

"Encounter With the Law," Kenyon Review, XVIII (Spring,
1956), 212-233. Collected in A Commodity of Dreams
and Other Stories.

"Beyond the Screen," Sewanee Review, LXV (Summer, 1957),
453. Collected in A Commodity of Dreams and Other
Stories.

"Delayed Hearing," Kenyon Review, XIX (Summer, 1957),
    448-462.   Collected in A Commodity of Dreams and Other
    Stories.
    Reprinted: Best American Short Stories, 1958, David
        Burnett, ed. Boston: Houghton, Mifflin, 1958.
            Pp. 215-230.

"A Secret Society," Virginia Quarterly Review, XXXIV (Sum-
    mer, 1958), 392-410.   Collected in A Commodity of
    Dreams and Other Stories.
    Reprinted: Best American Short Stories, 1959, David
        Burnett, ed. Boston: Houghton, Mifflin, 1959. Pp.
            18-36.

"Unbelievable Characters," Esquire, (September, 1959), 141.
    Reprinted: Best American Short Stories, 1960, David
        Burnett, ed. Boston: Houghton, Mifflin, 1960. Pp.
            218-229.

"From a Novel as Yet Untitled," Furioso, VI (Summer,
    1951), 11. (The main character's name, Felix Leger, is
    used for the pseudonymous main character in The Journal
    of the Fictive Life.)

"Escapist," Virginia Quarterly Review, XXVIII (Spring, 1962),
    263-275.

"Digressions Around a Crow," Carleton Miscellany, III
    (Spring, 1962), 38.

"The Idea of a University," Reporter, XXIX (October 10,
    1963), 46.

"The Nature of the Task," Virginia Quarterly Review, XLII
    (Spring, 1966), 234-243.

3.   Translations

"Dissertation 2, Canzone 1, First Ode from the Convivio,
    by Dante," Wake, X (1951), 98-100.
    Reprinted: Lyric Poetry of the Italian Renaissance,
        L. R. Lind, ed. New Haven: Yale University Press,
            1955. Pp. 163-164.
        Lyrics of the Middle Ages, Hubert Creekmore, ed.
            New York: Grove Press, 1959. Pp. 143-145.

4. Plays

"Cain," Tulane Drama Review, IV (Summer, 1959), 12-26.
    Collected in The Next Room of the Dream.

5. Essays

[Review of Robert Penn Warren's All the King's Men],
    Furioso, II (Fall, 1946), 69-70.

[Review of Mark Schorer's William Blake: The Politics of
    Vision], Furioso, II (Fall, 1946), 67-68.

"The Instruments of Irony," Furioso, II (Fall, 1946), 65-66.
    A review of John Crowe Ransom's Selected Poems.

"A Defense of, and a Proposal of Some Advantages to, Pub-
    lishers," Furioso, II (Fall, 1946), 38-49.
    An unsigned essay on the publishing world.

"The Agon of the Will as Idea," Furioso, II (Spring, 1947),
    29.
    An essay on Kenneth Burke.

"Low Thought," Furioso, III (Fall, 1947), 82-84.
    A review of Bend Sinister by Vladimir Nabokov.

"Summer's Flare and Winter's Thaw," Sewanee Review, LVI
    (Summer, 1948), 416-425. Collected in Poetry and Fic-
    tion: Essays.
    On John Crow Ransom's poetry.

"The Phoenix in the World: An Essay on Love's Parable by
    Robert Penn Warren," Furioso, III (Summer, 1948), 36-
    40.

"The Current of the Frozen Stream," Furioso, III (Fall,
    1948), 50-59. Collected in Poetry and Fiction: Essays.
    Reprinted: Sewanee Review, LXVII (Autumn, 1959), 585-
    597.
    An essay on the poetry of Allen Tate.

"A Survey of Criticism," Hudson Review, I (Autumn, 1948),
    411-419. Collected in Poetry and Fiction: Essays.
    A review of S. E. Hyman's The Armed Vision.

"The Poets," Kenyon Review, X (Summer, 1948), 501-507.
Review of five contemporary poets.

"Introduction to Your Career as an Author," Furioso, II
(Spring, 1949), 39-45. Unsigned essay.

"Passion and Form," Hudson Review, II (Autumn, 1949),
477-480.
A review of "The Diary of a Writer," by F. M. Does-
toevsky.

[A Review of Sleep in a Nest of Flames, by C. H. Ford],
Poetry, LXXVII (July, 1950), 234-238.

"High Thought," Furioso, V (Fall, 1950) 72-76.
A review of Kenneth Burke's A Rhetoric of Motives.

[A Review of The Little Blue Light, a play by Edmund Wil-
son], Furioso, V (Autumn, 1950), 71-72.

"Public Services and Pointing Hands," Sewanee Review, LIX
(Winter, 1951), 161-167. Collected in Poetry and Fic-
tion: Essays.
A review of two scholars' books on Shakespeare.

"Football," Furioso, VI (Spring, 1951), 66-68. Unsigned
essay.

"The Careful Poets and the Reckless Ones," Sewanee Review,
LX (Spring, 1952), 318-329. Collected in Poetry and
Fiction: Essays.
A review of eight contemporary poets.

"MacLeish and Viereck," Partisan Review, XX (January,
1953), 115-122. Collected in Poetry and Fiction: Essays.

"The Purgatorio as Drama," Sewanee Review, LXI (Summer,
1953), 500-506. Collected in Poetry and Fiction: Essays.
A review of Francis Fergusson's Dante's Drama of the
Mind.

"The Generation of Violence," Kenyon Review, XV (Summer,
1953), 477-483. Collected in Poetry and Fiction: Essays.
A review of The Collected Poems of Dylan Thomas.

"Three in One," Kenyon Review, XVI (Winter, 1954), 144-
154. Collected in Poetry and Fiction: Essays.

A review of Shapiro, Roethke, and Winters.

"Seven Poets and the Language," Sewanee Review, LXII
(Spring, 1954), 305-319. Collected in Poetry and Fiction:
Essays.
A review of seven contemporary poets.

"Contemporary Poets," Atlantic Monthly, CXCIV (September,
1954, 66-68.
A review of a pot pourri of modern poets.

"Poetry and Life: Lord Byron," Hudson Review, VII (Summer, 1954), 285-291. Collected in Poetry and Fiction:
Essays.
A review of a collection of Byron's letters and a biography of him.

"A Few Bricks from Babal," Sewanee Review, LXII (Autumn,
1954), 655-663. Collected in Poetry and Fiction: Essays.
A review of recent translations of The Fables of La Fon-
taine and Dante's Inferno.

"Just a Good Poet," Kenyon Review, XVIII (Winter, 1956),
131-136. Collected in Poetry and Fiction: Essays.
A review of Robert Graves.

"Sansom's Fictions," Kenyon Review, XVII (Winter, 1955),
130-135.
A review of three works by William Sansom.

"A Wild Civility," Kenyon Review, XVII (Summer, 1955),
477-484. Collected in Poetry and Fiction: Essays.
A review of new poems by Spender, Jarrell and Auden.

"The Marriage of Theseus and Hyppolyta," Kenyon Review,
XVIII, (Autumn, 1956), 633-640. Collected in Poetry and
Fiction: Essays.
An essay on A Midsummer-Night's Dream.

"The Poet and the Copy Writer: a Dialogue," Nation,
CLXXXIII (November 10, 1956), 402-406. Collected in
Poetry and Fiction: Essays.
A dialogue between the artist and the business man.

"Across the Woods and Into the Trees," Sewanee Review,
LXIII, (Autumn, 1955), 655-664. Collected in Poetry and
Fiction: Essays.

A review of Cowley's The Literary Situation, Blackmur's The Lion and the Honeycomb, and Eliseo Vivas' Creation and Discovery.

"Poems of Elizabeth Bishop," Poetry, LXXXVII (December, 1955), 179-181.

"The Poetry of Wallace Stevens," Sewanee Review, LXV (Winter, 1957), 1-15. Collected in Poetry and Fiction: Essays.

"The Morality of Art," Kenyon Review, XIX (Spring, 1957), 313-321. Collected in Poetry and Fiction: Essays. A review of Nabokov's Lolita and My Poor Robin.

"The Nature of Novels," Partisan Review, XXIV (Fall, 1957), 297-307. A review of seven contemporary novelists.

"The Discovery of Cozzens," Nation, CLXXXV (November 2, 1957), 306-308. Collected in Poetry and Fiction: Essays. A review of Cozzens' By Love Possessed.

"Younger Poets: The Lyric Difficulty," Kenyon Review, XX (Winter, 1958), 25-37. Collected in Poetry and Fiction: Essays. A review of seven contemporary poets.

"Iniquity it Is; But Pass the Can," Kenyon Review, XX, (Autumn, 1958), 642-644. Collected in Poetry and Fiction: Essays. A review of Norman Marlow's A. E. Houseman: Scholar and Poet.

"The Golden Compass Needle," Sewanee Review, LXVII (Winter, 1959), 94-109. Collected in Poetry and Fiction: Essays. A review of Seamarks by St. John Perse.

"The Swaying Form: A Problem in Poetry," Michigan Alumnus Quarterly Review, LXVI (Winter, 1959), 14-23. Collected in Poetry and Fiction: Essays. Reprinted: To the Young Writer, A. L. Bader, ed. Ann Arbor: University of Michigan Press, 1965. Pp. 105-121.

"The Ills from Missing Dates," Venture, III (Spring, 1959),

9-11. Collected in Poetry and Fiction: Essays.
A review of Nabokov's Nabokov's Dozen.

"The Poetry of Reed Whittemore," Kenyon Review, XXI
(Spring, 1959), 260-278. Collected in Poetry and Fiction:
Essays.

"Fiction Chronicle," Partisan Review, XXVII (Winter, 1960),
174-185. Collected in Poetry and Fiction: Essays.
A review of four contemporary novels.

"Meditations," Carleton Miscellany, I (Winter, 1960), 33-34.
On the nature of trees and poetry.

"The Dream of Reason, " Bennington College Bulletin, XXVII,
(February, 1960), 10-22. Collected in Poetry and Fiction: Essays.
Reprinted: Reporter, XXII (February 4, 1960), 29-33
(shorter form).
A reaction to social scientists' solutions to human problems.

"Thomas Mann's Faust Novel," Graduate Journal, III (Fall,
1960), 205-217. Collected in Poetry and Fiction: Essays.

"Themes and Methods in the Early Stories of Thomas Mann,"
Carleton Miscellany, II (Winter, 1961), 3-20. Collected
in Poetry and Fiction: Essays.

"True Moments in American Academic History," Carelton
Miscellany, II (Winter, 1961), 127-129.
On atrocities in literary criticism.

"The Muses Interest," Carleton Miscellany, IV (Spring,
1963), 83-90. Collected in Poetry and Fiction: Essays.
On writing poetry.

"The Bread of Faithful Speech--Wallace Stevens and the
Voices of Imagination," Carleton Miscellany, IV (Spring,
1963), 90-97. Collected in Poetry and Fiction: Essays.

"The Poems of Weldon Kees," Carleton Miscellany, II
(Spring, 1961), 89-93. Collected in Poetry and Fiction:
Essays.

"Composition and Fate in the Short Novel," Graduate Journal,
V (Winter, 1963), 375-391. Collected in Poetry and Fic-

tion: Essays.

"The Difficulty of Difficult Poetry," Carleton Miscellany, V
(Spring, 1964), 35-51.
An essay on understanding poetry.

"Attentiveness and Obedience," London Magazine, New Series
IV (November, 1964), 41-48. Collected in Poetry and
Fiction: Essays.
Nemerov answers the four questions he uses in Poets on
Poetry, concerning certain changes in poetry and the
effect of such hypothetical changes on his own poetry.

"Two Ways of the Imagination, A Study of Wordsworth and
Blake," Carleton Miscellany, V (Fall, 1964), 18-41.

"Bottom's Dream: The Likeness of Poems and Jokes,"
Virginia Quarterly Review, XLII (Autumn, 1966), 555-573.

"Other Vision," American Scholar, XXXV (Autumn, 1966),
720-723.
A response to the Spring, 1966 issue of American Scholar
which was devoted to the "Electric Revolution" and the
"Age of Circuitry."

"Speculative Equations: Poems, Poets and Computers,"
American Scholar, XXVI (Summer, 1967), 397-410.
The essay's theme is "Poetry in the New World of Ma-
chines."

"Howard Nemerov on Ben Belitt," Voyages, (Autumn, 1967),
29-30.

"On Going Down in History," Christian Century, LXXXV
(November 27, 1968), 1500-1501.
The future depends on the ability "to adapt our language
to reflect things as they are."

"On Metaphor," Virginia Quarterly Review, XLV (Autumn,
1969), 621-636.
Nemerov discusses two forms of magic on which poetry
builds.

"The Theory and Practice of What," Poetry, CXVI (April,
1970), 35-40.
In a critical review of the poetry anthology Naked Verse:
Recent American Poetry in Open Form, Nemerov con-

cludes the poetry and thus the anthology is narrow in
tone, subject and diction.

"An Occident Symposium," Occident, III (Summer, 1969),
101-113.
Nemerov and other poets answer the question "Is there
anything to like in contemporary literature?"

C.   COLLECTED MATERIAL REPRINTED IN ANTHOLOGIES

1.   Verse

"Glass Dialectic." Collected in The Image and the Law.
Reprinted: The War Poets, Oscar Williams, ed. New
York: John Day Company, 1945. P. 202.

"A Chromium-plated Hat," Collected in The Image and the
Law.
Reprinted: Fifteen Modern American Poets. George P.
Elliott, ed. New York: Holt, Rinehart and Winston,
1959, P. 107.

"History of a Literary Movement." Collected in The Image
and the Law and New and Selected Poems.
Reprinted: New Poets of England and America, Donald
Hall and Robert Pack, eds. New York: Meridian
Books, 1957. P. 224.
Five American Poets, Thom Gunn and Ted Hughes,
London: Faber and Faber, 1963. P. 35.
Poems on Poetry, Robert Wallace, ed. New York:
E. P. Dutton, 1965. P. 265.

"Sestina L." Collected in The Image and the Law.
Reprinted: The War Poets, Oscar Williams, ed. New
York: John Day Company, 1945. P. 203.

"Redeployment." Collected in Guide to the Ruins.
Reprinted: New Pocket Anthology of American Verse
From Colonial Days to the Present, Oscar Williams,
ed. New York: Pocket Books, 1955. P. 389.
Treasury of Jewish Poetry, Arthur Ausebel, ed.
New York: Crown Publishers, 1957. P. 132.
Five American Poets, Thom Gunn and Ted Hughes, eds.
London: Faber and Faber, 1963. P. 35.

This Land is Mine, Al Hine, ed.   New York: J. B.
  Lippincott, 1965.   P. 125.

"The Lives of Gulls and Children."   Collected in Guide to
  the Ruins.
  Reprinted: Fifteen Modern American Poets, George P.
     Elliott, ed.   New York: Holt, Rinehart and Winston,
     1959.   P. 110.
  New Poets of England and America, Donald Hall and
     Robert Pack, eds.   New York: Meridian Books,
     1957.   P. 251.

"The Ecstacies of Dialectic."   Collected in Guide to the
  Ruins.
  Reprinted: Fifteen Modern American Poets.   George P.
     Elliott, ed.   New York: Holt, Rinehart and Winston,
     1959.   P. 108.

"The Phoenix."   Collected in Guide to the Ruins and New
  and Selected Poems.
  Reprinted: New Pocket Anthology of American Verse
     From Colonial Days to the Present, Oscar Williams,
     ed.   New York: Pocket Books, 1955.   P. 390.

"Praising the Poets of That Country."   Collected in Guide
  to the Ruins.
  Reprinted: Poems on Poetry, Robert Wallace, ed.   New
     York: E. P. Dutton, 1965.   P. 64.

"The Quarry."   Collected in The Salt Garden.
  Reprinted: Art and Craft in Poetry, James Lape, ed.
     New York: Ginn and Company, 1967.   P. 58.

"Dandelions."   Collect in The Salt Garden and New and Selected Poems.
  Reprinted: New Pocket Anthology of American Verse
     From Colonial Days to the Present, Oscar Williams,
        ed.   New York: Holt, Rinehart and Winston, 1959.
        P. 112.
     Modern Verse in English, Allen Tate, ed.   New York:
        Macmillan and Company, 1958.   P. 622.
     Five American Poets, Thom Gunn and Ted Hughes, eds.
        London: Faber and Faber, 1963.   P. 43.

"The Winter Lightning."   Collected in The Salt Garden and
  The Winter Lightning.
  Reprinted: Modern Verse in English, Allen Tate, ed.

New York: Macmillan and Company, 1958. P. 112.
Five American Poets, Thom Gunn and Ted Hughes, eds.
    London: Faber and Faber, 1963. P. 622.

"The Goose Fish." Collected in The Salt Garden, New and
    Selected Poems and The Winter Lightning.
    Reprinted: New Poets in England and America, Donald
        Hall and Robert Pack, eds. New York: Meridian,
        1959. P. 247.
        Fifteen Modern American Poets, George P. Elliott, ed.
            New York: Holt, Rinehart and Winston, 1959.
            P. 121.
        Five American Poets, Thom Gunn and Ted Hughes, eds.
            London: Faber and Faber, 1963. P. 37.
        The Case for Poetry, Frederick Gwynn, et al.   New
            York: Prentice-Hall, 1965. P. 225.

"The Vacuum." Collected in The Salt Garden and New and
    Selected Poems.
    Reprinted: New Poets in England and America, Donald
        Hall and Robert Pack, eds. New York: Meridian,
        1957. P. 248.
        Five American Poets, Thom Gunn and Ted Hughes, eds.
            London: Faber and Faber, 1963. P. 37.

"Young Woman." Collected in The Salt Garden.
    Reprinted: Fifteen Modern American Poets, George P.
        Elliott, ed. New York: Holt, Rinehart and Winston,
        1959. P. 121.
        Erotic Poetry; The Lyrics, Ballads, Idyls and Epics
            of Love--Classical to Contemporary, William Cole,
            ed. New York: Random House, 1963. P. 68.

"The Snow Globe." Collected in The Salt Garden.
    Reprinted: Fifteen Modern American Poets, George P.
        Elliott, ed. New York: Holt, Rinehart and Winston,
        1959. P. 122.
        The Force of Few Words, Jacob Korg, ed. New York:
            Holt, Rinehart and Winston, 1966. P. 390.

"Suburban Prophecy." Collected in Mirrors and Windows.
    Reprinted: Art and Craft in Poetry, James Lape, ed.
    New York: Ginn and Company, 1967. P. 510.

"Mrs. Mandril." Collected in New and Selected Poems.
    Reprinted: Five American Poets, Thom Gunn and Ted
        Hughes, eds. London: Faber and Faber, 1963. P. 48.

"Mousemeal." Collected in New and Selected Poems.
  Reprinted: The Modern Poets, John Malcolm Brinnin and
    Bill Read, eds. New York: McGraw-Hill, 1963.
    P. 253.

"Lion & Honeycomb." Collected in The Next Room of the
  Dream.
  Reprinted: Poems on Poetry, Robert Wallace, ed. New
    York: E. P. Dutton, 1965. P. 94.

II. WORKS ABOUT HOWARD NEMEROV

A. BOOKS

1. Books about Howard Nemerov

Meinke, Peter. Howard Nemerov. Minneapolis: University
   of Minnesota Press, 1968.
   Meinke presents the most comprehensive published essay
   on Nemerov.

2. Contributions to Books

Beach, Joseph W. Obsessive Images. Minneapolis: University of Minnesota Press, 1960. Pp. 7-8, 9, 80, 299
   261.
   These sketchy discussions place Nemerov in the main-
   stream of the poetry of the 1940's.

Burnett, Whit and Hallie. The Modern Short Story in the
   Making. New York: Hawthorn Publishers, 1964. Pp.
   303-304.
   Burnett gives an account of the collaboration with W. R.
   Johnson on the short story "Exchange of Men" and a
   comment on Nemerov's use of point of view.

Dickey, James. Babel to Byzantium. New York: Faraar,
   Straus and Giroux, 1968. Pp. 35-41.
   The essay is a chatty, imprecise appreciation of Howard
   Nemerov.

Harvey, R. D. "A Prophet Armed: an Introduction to the
   Poetry of Howard Nemerov," in Poets in Progress, H. B.
   Hungerford, ed. , Chicago: Northwestern University
   Press, 1967, Pp. 116-133.
   The discussion of the themes of war, city, and nature,
   which also distinguishes between satire and serious
   lyrics, makes a well documented defense of Nemerov's
   canon.

Rosenthal, M. L. The Modern Poets. New York: Oxford
     University Press, 1960. Pp. 255-261.
     Nemerov's poetry's "chief contribution is in its hypotheti-
          cal, liberal-tinged commitment to whatever positive
          can be wrung out of the 'things of this world.' "

     _____. The New Poets. New York: Oxford University
     Press, 1967. Pp. 310-311.
     "Nemerov is one of a number of poets whom we might
          call 'independents,' though the term would be something
          of a misnomer. It is easy enough to see their place
          in the whole modern picture; they are independents in
          the sense that they have worked on their own, in the
          manner of many artists, without being closely involved
          with the momentary centers of most intense poetic in-
          fluence and perhaps without attracting much critical at-
          tention. "

Smith, Dora, et al. American Experience: Poetry. New
     York: Macmillan, 1968. P. 344.
     "Nemerov does not expect to solve the human dilemma
          . . . he either exposes it, acknowledges it, or tries
          to identify some recognizable shape and positive value
          within the wide confusion. "

Unger, Leonard, ed. Seven Modern American Poets. Min-
     neapolis: University of Minnesota Press, 1967. Pp. 256-
     261.
     Unger finds Nemerov similar to Allen Tate.

Waggoner, Hyatt. American Poets From the Puritans to the
     Present. New York: Houghton, Mifflin Company, 1968.
     Pp. xv, 543, 597, 610-613, 694.
     Quoting too extensively from Nemerov's own self-analysis,
          Waggoner finds Nemerov a neo-romantic.

B. UNPUBLISHED ESSAYS

Knight, Linda Jean. "A Study of Howard Nemerov's Lan-
     guage as it Reflects the Theme of Time in His Poetry. "
     Unpublished Master's thesis, Department of English,
     University of Vermont, 1967.

Meinke, J. Peter. "The Writings of Howard Nemerov, " Un-
     published Ph. D. dissertation, University of Minnesota,
     1966.

C.   PERIODICAL ARTICLES

Benoit, Raymond. "The New American Poetry," Thought,
     XLIV (Summer, 1969), 200-218.
     The poetry of Nemerov, Snyder, Stafford and Wilber re-
     vives the romantic tradition.

Chester, Ellen. "Nemerov Proves Himself Poet and Astute
     Self-Critic." Vassar Miscellany News, L (March 9,
     1966), 2-3.
     The short review of a poetry reading, offers a bit of a
     character sketch.

Gerstenberger, Donna. "An Interview with Howard Nemerov,"
     Trace, #35 (January, 1960), 22-25.
     The interview covers poetry, educational problems, and
     recent trends in poetry.

Hopkins, John. "Poet Writes Because He 'Can't Not,'"
     Collegian (Student Newspaper, University of Vermont)
     April 17, 1964, 3.
     Hopkins gives an account of a poetry reading and a slight
     interview.

Randall, Julia. "Genius of the Shore: The Poetry of How-
     ard Nemerov," Hollins Critic, VI (June, 1969), 1-12.
     Miss Jarrell speaks of Nemerov's double vision which
     makes "language live by confronting things with the in-
     nocent mind of an Adam, by naming them to themselves
     afresh through the powers of the mind which is some-
     how continuous with them;" and by doing so, Miss Jar-
     rell makes Nemerov a prophet.

Skully, James. "The Audience Swam for Their Lives,"
     Nation, CXCVIII (March 9, 1964), 244.
     Skully's review is of a YM-YWHA-sponsored-symposium
     on "The State of American Poetry Today" in which
     Nemerov participated.

D.   BOOK REVIEWS

The Image and the Law

Arrowsmith, William. "Recent verse," Hudson Review, I
     (Spring, 1948), 100-101.

"I cannot help but think that the blame lies in Nemerov's
failure to provide . . . significant integrity by making
his myth his own: whose image, whose law?"

Berryman, John. "Waiting for the End, Boys," Partisan
Review, XV (February, 1948), 260.
Berryman finds Nemerov very much influenced by the
"Auden climate."

"Briefly Noted," New Yorker, XXIII (November 15, 1947),
133.
" . . . he is the sort of writer who might never have
turned to poetry unless he had been encouraged by certain anti-Romantic essays of the Early Eliot or by
Valerey's stern dictum 'Enthusiasm is not an artist's
state of mind.'"

Crane, Milton. "Eye and the Mind," New York Times,
August 10, 1947, "Book Review" sec., p. 10.
"Howard Nemerov has attempted to read unity into his
first book of poems by giving it the title The Image
and the Law which, he says, 'exposes the conflict and
theme of the poems: the ever present dispute between
eye and that of the mind.' The portentousness of this
statement is reflected in the poems themselves, which
unfortunately show unity of conception such as their author attributes to them."

Furioso I (Fall, 1947), 164.
The magazine gives a humorous review by Nemerov's
fellow editors.

Golffing, F. C. "Question of Strategy," Poetry, LXXI
(November, 1947), 94-97.
Golffing finds illusory the dichotomy between the two ways
of looking at the world and that therefore the poetry
suffers as it jousts with windmills.

MacLeish, Fleming. "Dichotomic Verse," Saturday Review,
XXX (November 1, 1947), 38.
"Mr. Nemerov, in his effort to achieve what is fresh, incisive and concise, sometimes produces involutions and
contortions which are often unmusical and generally difficult."

The Melodramatists

Barrows, Herbert. "Satirized Segments," New York Times,
     April 3, 1949, "Book Review" sec. , p. 4.
     "His satire would have been more effective if it had been
     less heavy handed. "

Brandel, Marc. "Logical Nonsense in Boston Setting," Phila-
     delphia Inquirer, April 17, 1949, "Books" sec. , p. 8.
     "Like a plum pudding, Howard Nemerov's first novel is
     not an unpalatable mixture of seemingly ill assorted in-
     gredients. "

Broyard, Anatole. "To Say and Say Not," Partisan Review,
     XVI (May, 1949), 551.
     "Mr. Nemerov's excitations are irresistable and charming-
     ly autonomous, which makes this novel brilliant and
     provocative though it is a technical failure."

Bardin, J. F. "An Amatory Investigation," New Leader,
     XXXII (August 6, 1949), 8.
     Bardin gives an analysis of the paradox which he sees
     controlling the novel.

"Briefly Noted," New Yorker, XXV (April 9, 1949), 120.
     "The writing is sometimes witty, sometimes densely cryp-
     tic, and sometimes warmed-over Huxley. "

Bullock, F. H. "Brahmins," New York Herald Tribune,
     April 3, 1949, "Book Review" sec. , p. 14.
     Bullock finds the novel is " 'cups of a pale, lemony
     punch, which tasted somewhat vicious and medicinal,
     nastier than it needed . . . ' "

Cotter, Joseph. Best Sellers, IX (May, 1949), 42.
     "Mr. Nemerov has encouraging possibilities as a stylist
     in satire. "

Crane, Milton. Chicago Review, III (Spring, 1949), 7.
     "The central question which is raised by Howard Neme-
     rov's first novel, The Melodramatists, and which must
     dominate any discussion of the book, is an ancient and
     vexing one: what becomes of a satire that fails to be
     recognized as such because of the ineptitude of the
     writer or the obtuseness of the audience. "

Farrelly, John. "Fiction Parade," New Republic, CXX
    (May 9, 1949), 26.
    "There's a metaphor among all this which describes the
        novel: Time (read The Melodramatists) is a 'desert
        in which the lineaments of decisive acts crumble or
        got covered, lost, in sand.' "

Hunter, A. C. Savannah, Georgia News, April 10, 1949,
    p. 4.
    "One of the prerogatives of superior wit is the privilege
        to ridicule, more politely termed satirize, and Howard
        Nemerov lives up to his reputation as an editor of
        Furioso to upsurp this privilege with a vengeance."

Kapp, Isa. "A Lively Irreverence," Commentary, VI (June,
    1949), 613.
    "(The Melodramatists) takes the position that, in the
        midst of the fragmentary and the dissonant, it is pos-
        sible to preserve one's identity and make a productive
        start."

Kirkus, XVII (February 1, 1949), 67.
    "A generally unattractive account which might--in its
        cerebral cleaverness--qualify for a few."

L., E. A. "Beware This Satire About Boston," Boston
    Globe, April 3, 1949, Sec. A, p. 29.
    "It is hilarious with the hilarity that is close to tragedy;
        certainly tragedy is being pointed at by using hilarity
        that is akin to hysteria."

MacGregor, Martha. "Boston Was Never Like This," New
    York Post Home News, May 18, 1949, p. 28.
    "The theme which underlies the rather incredible plot is
        the search for security in a corrupt and senseless
        world."

Matthews, Clayton. Huntington Park, California Bulletin,
    July 21, 1949, p. 8.
    The book "is the most depressing study of moral decay
        and degeneracy, possibly excepting The Little Foxes,
        this writer has ever seen."

Minton, R. W. "Bostonians Can be Improper, at Least in
    Melodramatists," New York World Telegram, April 12,
    1949, p. 26.
    "What began as a plot imitative of Evelyn Waugh finally

deteriorates into one reminiscent of Thorne Smith . . ."

Peyton, Green. "Diabolical Chronicle Overreaches its
   Mark," Dallas, Texas News, April 24, 1949, Sec. 6,
   p. 7.
   "He finds the soul of man obsessed by a suicidal urge,
   and his reaction is to offer it a gun."

Prescott, Orville. New York Times, April 5, 1949, p. 27.
   "It is a curious paradox that, although The Melodramatists is unsuccessful as a whole, considered as satire
   or as humor, it yet conveys an impression of brilliance
   and talent."

Rolo, Charles. "The Doctor and the Bishop," Atlantic
   Monthly, CLXXXIII (June, 1949), 89.
   The novel is a "saturation bombardment which flattens
   every target in sight and leaves one wondering just
   what strategic purpose has been served."

San Francisco Chronicle, June 5, 1949, "This World" sec.,
   p. 24.
   " 'Over-sympathy' has the unforeseen result occasionally
   of dulling the edge of the author's wit; adulatory
   chronicle becomes too enmeshed in the satire, at the
   expense of the latter."

Shumaker, M. B. "Howard Nemerov's Fine First Novel is
   Fluent Satire," Washington, D. C. Star, April 17, 1949,
   Sec. C, p. 3.
   "It is somewhat regrettable that the satire is equally
   trenchant throughout . . ."

Smith, Harrison. "Two Fall From Grace," Saturday Review, XXXII (April 2, 1949), 17.
   "The Melodramatists is true satire, written in the spirit
   of comedy."

Trilling, Diana. "Fiction in Review," Nation, CLXVIII
   (May 7, 1949), 537.
   "I know of no better index to our immediately contemporary culture--or at least to that section of it which is
   consciously devoted to ideas."

Villafranca, Suzanne. "Too Much Freedom Wrecks Sisters
   in Depressing Novel," New Haven Register, April 17,
   1949, Sec. 4, p. 6.

"Brilliantly shallow."

Wasson, Donald. Library Journal, LXXIV (March 1, 1949),
     337.
     "Apparently an attempt to contrast the empirical with the
        pragmatic in modern life . . ."

Wright, J. A. "Melodramatists More Melo than Mellow,"
     Los Angeles Mirror, April 2, 1949, p. 12.
     " . . . upon rereading it, the last vestige of human de-
        cency is ground into the cigaret butts and broken
        whisky glasses of Nemerov's conclusions."

Young, Allen. "Writer Shows Another Aspect of Boston
     Life," Denver Post, April 3, 1949, Sec. C, p. 4.
     Nemerov is "a contemporary Hogarth . . . His temper
        seems sometimes distant but it may be argued that he
        is with purpose intensifying his moral passion to gain
        a fresh sense of values from which to observe and on
        which to act."

Guide to the Ruins

Allen, Morse. "Fouler Shapes," Hartford Currant, May 21,
     1950, p. 14.
     "Mr. Nemerov in his disorder has produced these poems,
        and anyone who wishes to share his general dis-
        gruntledness should read them."

Brennan, J. P. "Soars Some, Shuffles Much," New Haven
     Register, June 18, 1950, Sec. 4, p. 8.
     "It appears to me that Nemerov is too often carried
        away by his subject matter."

Brooks, Gwendolyn. "Poetry Studded with Delight," Chicago
     News, May 17, 1950, p. 38.
     Brooks' review concentrates on Nemerov's poetic tech-
        niques.

Bryson, Artemisa B. "Distinguishing Marks of Poetry,"
     Fort Worth Star Telegram, October 1, 1950, Sec. 2,
     p. 3.
     "We are struck by a bitter note of disillusionment and an
        impatient, almost contemptuous treatment of his sub-
        ject."

Columbus, Ohio Dispatch, May 14, 1950, Sec. E, p. 15.
    "Dissembled in many mediums, some of them less heroic
        than stone, time may be said to constitute the leit-
        motif of this volume."

Crane, Milton.   "Alive to Agony," New York Times, May
    5, 1950, "Book Review" Sec., p. 12.
    "The besetting sin of these poems is not trickery, but
        ellipsis."

Daiches, David.   "Some Recent Poetry," Yale Review, XL
    (Winter, 1951), 356.
    Daiches finds "A curious emptiness . . . generalized
        imagery which does not appear to be wedded together
        by a dominating vision . . . Too many of the poems
        lack a burning core to mould the pattern and imagery
        of the whole into a compelling shape."

Eberhart, Richard.   "Five Poets," Kenyon Review, XIV
    (Winter, 1952), 168.
    "He is intellectual rather than sensuous, but something of
        both."

Gram, W. P.   "Four Minor Modern Poets," Voices, #143
    (Autumn, 1950), 317.
    "Nemerov is concerned with the symptoms and parapher-
        nalia of living, as expressed through myth and with
        man's futility against time, both ancient and present."

Hall, James.   "Ordered Withdrawals," Virginia Quarterly
    Review, XXVI (Summer, 1950), 464.
    ". . . in Guide to the Ruins, Nemerov's best poems,
        presumably his latest, set up a distance of myth and
        ceremonial form against this sympathy-craving human-
        ity . . ."

Jarrell, Randall.   "The Profession of Poetry," Partisan
    Review, XVII (September, 1950), 725-726.
    Jarrell finds "a dry plainness and hardness, a 'classical'
        stiffness and severity."

Kirkus, XVIII (April 1, 1950), 224.
    "For those who can take Kafka straight."

Koch, Viviene.   "The Necessary Angels of Earth," Sewanee
    Review, LIX (Autumn, 1951), 674.
    "While I do not think we can expect any enlargement of

the capacity for sensuous apprehension--that first gift
to the poet is given and not earned--his sincerity and
his sharp intellectual control will, no doubt, reap their
proper increments."

Morgan, Frederick. "Three Poets," Hudson Review, III
(Autumn, 1950), 463.
"What I chiefly miss is a center of gravity or of force,
the sense of a strong controlling sensibility."

M., W. B. T. "Impelling Irony," Cincinnati Times-Star,
May 20, 1950, "Book Talk" Sec., p. 8.
"He shouts warnings of an incipient and punitive mad-
ness."

Salomon, I. L. "Corruption and Metaphysics," Saturday
Review, XXXIII (July 1, 1950), 33.
"Howard Nemerov suffers from poetic schizophrenia."

Scott, W. T. "Some New Poetry," Providence, R.I. Journal,
July 9, 1950, Sec. 6, p. 8.
"So much of it is, in his own phrase, 'the furnished
room, the garment without seam.' "

Shulenberger, Arvid. Poetry, LXXVI (1950), 368-370.
Howard Nemerov is concerned with "the ruins of a postwar world."

Smith, Harry. "Mr. Nemerov's Recent Verse," New
Leader, XXXIII (November 13, 1950), 22.
" . . . an academic mastery of the superficial techniques
of modernism does not insure good or interesting poetry."

Southworth, J. G. Toledo Blade, June 25, 1950, Sec. 2,
p. 5.
Nemerov "reveals that he is aware of the 'new' criticism
and has profited by it."

U.S. Quarterly Book Review, VI (September, 1950), 287.
"Having apparently gone to school to Yeats and the Eliza-
bethans, the poet knows how to create an effective
sort of counterpoint by manipulating dramatic rhetorical rhymes on the one hand, and lyrical refrains and
other musical devices on the other . . . "

West, Ray B. "Contemporary Poets," Western Review, XVI

(Spring, 1951), 76.
"His attitude is quietly mocking, but not without envy."

Wharton, Will. "Clear But Gloomy Verse," Saint Louis
    Post Dispatch, May 18, 1950, Sec. E, p. 22.
    "The poems have a kind of religious and prophetic fervor,
        but their uniformly querulous and carping tone eventu-
        ally becomes monotonous."

Federigo, or The Power of Love

Betsky, Seymour. "Some Notes on Recent American
    Novels," Essays in Criticism, [Oxford], VI (January,
    1956), 105.
    "The book is marred by the kind of drift to epigram that
        depends for its effect on the reader's knowing about
        little magazine Freud and Marx: the American New
        Critic Doing a Novel."

B., J. L. Worcester, Massachusetts Telegram, October 10,
    1954, p. 6.
    " . . . this is the work of a man whose writing is so
        hampered by the esoteric and so clogged with atrophied
        wit as to be almost incomprehensible."

_____. Boston Post, September 26, 1954, Sec. A, p. 8.
    "Mr. Nemerov brings too 'highbrow,' too dry an ap-
        proach to a human problem. His writing is without
        feeling, cold, clinical and reflects, alas, the influence
        of some of the esoteric journals for which he has writ-
        ten."

E., H. S. "Satire on Marriage is Insane, Boring," New
    Bedford, Massachusetts Standard-Times, September 19,
    1954, p. 7.
    "A writer of Mr. Nemerov's obvious craftmanship should
        devote himself to worthier subjects."

"Fiction Briefly Noted," New Yorker, XXX (October 16,
    1954), 162.
    "A cold, very mannered, very amusing story, of the game
        of sex as it is played by some idle-hearted, wilful,
        youngish New York men and women, all of whom have
        enough money or wit to provide a bright, brittle at-
        mosphere for Mr. Nemerov's ironic romp."

Kincheloe, H. G.   "A Blend Produces Brilliant Novel,"
   Raleigh, North Carolina News Observer, September 26,
   1954, Sec. 4, p. 5.
   "Perhaps Mr. Nemerov's attitude toward his characters
      and the world they inhabit is best suggested by his de-
      scription of Julian near the end of the story as being
      'bemused by the idea that life was one grand theatri-
      cal performance.' "

Lyon, William.   "Advertising and Modern Life Gets Satirical Shellacking," Norfolk, Virginia Pilot, September 26,
   1954, Sec. 3, p. 10.
   Nemerov is "not mad at the world so much as puzzled
      by it."

McLaughlin, Richard.   "Modern Marriage Without Meaning,"
   Springfield, Massachusetts Republican, September 26,
   1956, Sec. C, p. 9.
   "Mr. Nemerov has written one of those formless fiction-
      al essays which has the clever practically legerdemain
      effect of suggesting he is something more than a verb-
      al juggler."

Minton, Robert.   "Intellectual Joke," Saturday Review,
   XXXVII (November 13, 1954), 57.
   "Mr. Nemerov sees life in contrapuntal terms.   For
      every positive there is a negative."

Mizener, Arthur.   "Fiction Chronicle," Sewanee Review,
   LXIII (Summer, 1955), 484.
   "Mr. Nemerov's subject is the ambiguity of reality and
      he is interested in what happens, not in the usual
      sense, but in the sense Sir Thomas Brown had in mind
      when he said that man is the only true amphibian and
      lives in divided and distinguished worlds."

Morton, Frederic.   "A Motley of Masques," New York
   Herald Tribune, October 3, 1954, "Book Review" Sec.,
   p. 12.
   "Federigo, in brief, constitutes an elegant potpourri
      of novelistic designs, a piquantly conceived, finely
      written and philosophically mannered motley of mas-
      ques in modern dress, not in cohesive story."

Pickerel, Paul.   Yale Review, New Series, XLIV (Autumn,
   1954), xviii.
   "He does not love his characters; they are always threat-

ening to bore him. Only when he gets them under the
scalpel is he completely at ease . . . "

Rolo, Charles. "Manhattan Madness," Atlantic Monthly,
    CXCIV (November, 1954), 96.
    The novel "reveals him as a comic artist of real origin-
        ality. "

Roscoe, Gerald. "An Academic Amused by the World,"
    Boston Globe, October 10, 1954, Sec. A, p. 5.
    "As he sees it, this is a world of neurotics, maybe psy-
        chotics. "

San Francisco Chronicle, November 14, 1954, "Books" Sec.,
    p. 27.
    The novel is "a ribald little feather about sophisticated
        New Yorkers. Its effect is like a sip of absinthe to
        the uninitiated. "

West, Herbert. "Quite, Quite Unhappy," New York Times,
    September 26, 1954, "Book Review" Sec., p. 4.
    The novel is " . . . in a Waughish sort of way, a rath-
        er hilarious pastiche with serious undertones. "

West, Ray B. "The Unities of Modern Fiction," Kenyon
    Review, XVII (Spring, 1955), 326-329.
    The novel reflects "what has become a tendency in re-
        cent American fiction to avoid social realism and to
        adopt a kind of surrealistic formalism as a means of
        expressing modern life. "

The Salt Garden

Booklist, LI (March 15, 1955), 294.
    "Cerebral and somewhat detached poems about the mod-
        ern predicament by a poet who apparently rates logic
        and formal perfection higher than emotion. "

Burke, Kenneth. "Comments on Eighteen Poems by Howard
    Nemerov," Sewanee Review, LX (January, 1952), 117-
    131.
    Burke's essay is an appreciative reading of "The Scales
        of the Eyes" which accompanied the poem in its first
        printing.

Carruth, Hayden. "Seven Books in Search of a Customer,"

Poetry, LXXXVI (June, 1955), 169.
"The most constant analogue is salt . . . "

Cotten, L. A. "A Rising Young Poet is Analyzed," Char-
lotte, North Carolina Observer, April 24, 1955, Sec. B,
p. 5.
"He speaks with controlled passion and troubled insight
into the mystery of things which seems to be his chief
theme; and his mastery of irregular but balanced
rythms, half-rhymes, and stanza patterns give strong
artistic form to material that might otherwise be
amorphous and even inarticulate. "

Dickey, James. "Some of All of It," Sewanee Review,
LXIV (Spring, 1956), 333-336.
Dickey finds that Nemerov is apt to become, of his own
choice, stereotyped into the Auden-Eliot-Yeats tradition.

Fisher, J. A. "Six Younger Poets," Mandala, I (Spring,
1956), 134.
"The wit saves the volume even when Mr. Nemerov gets
carried away with his technical skills and seeks merely to impress. "

Fitts, Dudly. "Poetry Chronicle," Partisan Review, XXII
(Fall, 1955), 542-548.
"The greater part of his book is an exercise in silent
writing.

Hillyer, Robert. "A Dark, Bleak Spaciousness," New York
Times, July 17, 1955, "Book Review" Sec. , p. 4.
"The general mood is dark, sometimes as forbidding as
a frozen plain that thaws, but does not bloom, under
occasional sunlight. "

Jarrell, Randall. "Recent Poetry," Yale Review, New Series, LXV (Autumn, 1955), 126-128.
Though Jarrell finds the poetry good, he finds Yeats' influence on Nemerov regrettable.

Jerome, Judson. "Hard Eloquence," Dayton, Ohio News,
May 1, 1955, Sec. C, p. 3.
"It is characteristic of Nemerov's hard-bitten art to give
us the deepest emotion stripped to the bone. "

Kirkus, XXII (December 1, 1954), 801.

"One wonders how with so little passion he can go much
   further than he has. For he seems to have little to
   express other than a rather wry skepticism."

MacDonald, G. D. Library Journal, LXXX (April 1, 1955),
   813.
   "The poems are contemplative, dwelling most often on
   change in nature and endurance in man."

Morse, Samuel French. "Two Poets," Hartford, Connecti-
   cut Courant, July 3, 1955, "Magazine" Sec., p. 19.
   "It may be, too, that Mr. Nemerov's self-consciously
   disciplined approach to poetry will pay more dividends
   in the long run than a reliance upon originality and a
   cultivation of disarming idiosyncracies."

Philbrick, C. H. "Poetry: Auden, Spender, and Three
   Americans," Providence, Rhode Island Journal, May 1,
   1955, Sec. 6, p. 8.
   "Mr. Nemerov's discovery in this book is the shore between land and sea, self and time."

Stocking, D. M. "The Delightful Poems of Morley . . .
   And Other New Books of Verse," San Francisco Chronicle, April 10, 1955, p. 21.
   Howard Nemerov "generally starts from a situation, often a natural event, which he presents with palpable
   sensuous reality, then draws from it his meditation."

U. S. Quarterly Book Review, XI (September, 1955), 355.
   "Although he is still an ironist and satirist, his writing
   has acquired a purity of seriousness that changes the
   familiar posture into something much more authentic."

Untermeyer, Louis. "Variegated Verse," Saturday Review,
   XXXVIII (May 21, 1955), 15.
   "Unfortunately, Mr. Nemerov has not quite made up his
   mind what kind of poet he wants to be."

Mirrors and Windows

Ciardi, John. Saturday Review, XLI (September 27, 1958),
   18.
   "His range is wide, his control excellent, and his concern always the central one of finding the place of
   value in the real world."

Fitts, Dudly. "With a Moralizing Public Tone," New York
    Times, February 8, 1959, "Book Review" Sec., p. 10.
    Fitts finds a "portentous assumption of the moralizing
        public tone" counterpointed by "the passionate verity
        of the writing when its verse becomes poetry."

Flint, F. Cudworth. "Seeing, Thinking, Saying, Singing,"
    Virginia Quarterly Review, XXXV (1959), 310.
    Flint finds the core of the poems in the metaphysical
        problem of flux, for our "universe (is) composed of
        events and transactions between them; 'things have dis-
        integrated.' "

Gunn, Thom. "Seeing and Thinking," American Scholar,
    XVIII (Summer, 1959), 394-396.
    "The effect of the writing is far more complex than that
        of a simply visual impression . . . there is suggested
        --rather than a 'picture,' rather than an experience--
        a whole category of experience, in the evocation of
        which judgment is inevitably involved. Yet the judg-
        ment is not mere moralizing."

Kizer, Carolyn. "Nemerov: The Middle of the Journey,"
    Poetry, XCIII (December, 1958), 178.
    "The poet, engaged in the sunlit nightmare of the con-
        temporary world, both hotly observes it and coolly
        notes it down."

Mercier, Vivian. "Development of the Poetic Personality,"
    Commonweal, LXIX (February 13, 1959), 523.
    "Nemerov may not wear his heart on his sleeve . . .
        but--make no mistake--he has one."

Dallas Times Herald, September 14, 1958, "Roundup" Sec.,
    p. 17.
    "He begins with intensely perceived sights and sounds and
        ends in acute commentary--dry, equable, and thus
        doubly penetrating."

Philbrick, C. H. "Howard Nemerov," Providence, Rhode
    Island Journal, July 27, 1958, Sec. W, p. 14.
    "Sinewy, astringent, and possessed of an honest pathos
        as well as a voice that can sing to its own tune, he
        is a poet who is on his way."

Ray, David. "An Opening Door for Poetry," Western Re-
    view, XXIII (Spring, 1959), 287-288.

"The capacity for the larger reflection, the power of rais-
ing the image into a philosophic speculation, distinguishes Nemerov from much that is competent in poetry."

Rosenthal, M. L. "False Wentletrap! Avaunt," Nation,
CLXXXII (August 16, 1958), 75.
Rosenthal finds that the theme is that "the subjective life
cannot finally be distinguished from the 'real' life of
the world around us or from the mind's projection of
the ideal."

Rosten, Norman. Venture, III (Spring, 1959), 75-77.
"This new volume by Howard Nemerov is called Mirrors
and Windows: mirrors to catch the sharp reflections
of one's face, windows to look out upon the wider landscape of man in context with nature and history. Or,
to those probing for a future symbolism, we have a
double glass: one deflecting, reminding of the personal
impasse, the other allowing us to see through and freely beyond."

Squires, Radcliffe. "Faces and Voices," Northwest Review,
II (Spring, 1959), 87.
"Both window and mirror, observation and imagination,
common sense and sensitivity characterize the best
poems in the collection. And the best ones seem to
be some of the truest poetry of our time."

Thompson, John. "Just a Bit of This and That," Hudson
Review, II (Autumn, 1958), 446.
Nemerov "has mastered a style that is relaxed and reflective; his poems are certainly 'as well-written as
prose.' "

Whittemore, Reed. "Observations of an Alien" New Republic, CXXXVIII (June 23, 1958), 27.
The essay is on Nemerov in general and the collection in
particular, focusing on the themes of alienation and
identity.

Wright, James. "Some Recent Poetry," Sewanee Review,
LXVI (Fall, 1958), 666-668.
Wright finds basic in Nemerov a sense that "the natural
world can be beautiful because it is indifferent."

The Homecoming Game

Baker, M. L.   "Man of Ideas Confronts A Need to Act,"
    Columbus, Ohio Dispatch, March 24, 1957, "Tab" Sec.,
    p. 10.
    The reader must "steer his way through the numerous
        allusions to zeitgeist, the Hegelian synthesis, 'la
        trahison des clercs,' and other philosophical concepts
        of the types so dear to the academic mind."

Beck, Warren.   "He Places Ivory Tower at Ethical Cross-
    roads," Chicago Tribune, March 10, 1957, Sec. 4, p. 11.
    Nemerov "shows how truth and justice are come by only
        piecemeal . . . "

Buchan, Jim.   "Two Satires Too Pseudo," Norman, Okla-
    homa Daily Oklahoman, May 19, 1957, "Magazine" Sec.,
    p. 23.
    Nemerov's novel "fails to achieve as much as it might
        because the writer gets involved in verbage, technique,
        and message."

Bullock, F. H.   "Conflict and Chicanery on the Campus,"
    New York Herald Tribune, March 3, 1957, "Book Re-
    view," Sec., p. 5.
    Nemerov "indulges himself in over elaborate phrasing."

Cleveland Plain Dealer, April 21, 1957, Sec. G, p. 8.
    Nemerov is a "literary mannerist . . . the writing, too,
        tends to become excessively precious as if the author
        no longer knew quite where he was going."

Crane, Milton.   Saturday Review, XL (April 27, 1957), 27.
    Crane finds the characters and actions implausible and
        therefore unsatisfactory.

Davedeit, G. C.   "A Professor Finds He is as Other Men,"
    Washington, D. C. Post Times Herald, March 10, 1957,
    Sec. E, p. 7.
    "In a cosmos where, as the vernacular describes it, one
        thing leads to another, man can but follow.   In all
        probability, though, he will gesture as he does so, and
        there both his (Nemerov's and man's) humanity and his
        comedy lie."

Elliot, George P.   "Fiction Chronicle," Hudson Review,

X (Summer, 1957), 293.
" . . . in The Homecoming Game so much energy seems
    to go into tooling the plot that little is left over for a
    better purpose."

Garber, Mary. "Professor's Football Woe Funny, True,"
    Winston-Salem, North Carolina Journal and Sentinel,
    March 17, 1957, p. 18.
    "It's good, but its not quite good enough."

Hayes, Richard. "Cheerful Lobotomy," Commonweal, LXIX
    (March 6, 1959), 600.
    "The Homecoming Game distills out of such cool wisdom
    of imperfection a very real secular terror, and only a
    certain determinism in the pattern--a pale, harsh clar-
    ity which Mr. Nemerov would be the first to admit as
    the coast and the climate of solitary reason--denies it
    a more resonant power."

Mizener, Arthur. "Spring Fiction," Kenyon Review, XIX
    (Summer, 1957), 492.
    "For the most part the book is solidly created and full of
    the authority of acute observation."

Morrison, Don. " 'Tall Story' was Painless Play," Minne-
    apolis Tribune, February 8, 1959, Sec. E, p. 7.
    Morrison presents an interview with Nemerov about the
    play made from The Homecoming Game.

Poore, Charles. New York Times, February 28, 1957, p.
    25.
    "Suave, brilliant, and entertaining, but it really does not
    add up to anything much whatever when all is said and
    done."

Reagan, Michael D. "Organization Gothic," Nation,
    CLXXXIV (June 4, 1957), 396.
    The "book illustrated the difficulty of maintaining moral
    values (or even being certain that they are involved)
    in the face of an amoral insistence that success, un-
    derstanding and the 'good of the institution' are the
    important things."

Rolo, Charles. Atlantic, CXCIX (May, 1957), 86.
    Howard Nemerov dramatizes with "feeling, humor, and
    precision."

Sullivan, Richard. "He Flunked the Star," New York Times,
   March 3, 1957, "Book Review" Sec., p. 5.
   "A slip or two could have turned this novel into bur-
      lesque, but there are no slips."

Wassmer, T. A. Best Sellers, XVII (April 15, 1957), 29.
   "It is a real adventure in wisdom to realize appreciative-
      ly the prudential judgments of others in moral situa-
      tions. This is the one theme of The Homecoming
      Game."

White, R. L. "The Trying Out of The Homecoming Game,"
   Colorado Quarterly, X (Spring, 1959), 84.
   White compares the movie adaptation and the novel.

A Commodity of Dream and Other Stories

Beck, Warren. "Fourteen Ingenious Stories," Chicago
   Tribune, March 8, 1959, Sec. 4, p. 3.
   "Several tales end in violence, which may seem an arbi-
      trary resolution of plot, but elucidates a recurring
      subject, the movement of some strained mind into the
      ultimate eccentricity of a desperate blow."

Blakeston, Oswell. "New Novels," Time and Tide, XLI
   (March 5, 1960), 260.
   "The makeweights are too light."

"Briefly Noted," New Yorker, XXXV (March 14, 1959), 166.
   "Most of the stories are fixed in no particular time, but
      they are all fixed in their own special locality."

Conroy, Jack. "Seething in Teacups," Chicago Times,
   April 12, 1959, Sec. 3, p. 4.
   The stories "indicate that modern man is more often de-
      feated by mosquito bites on the spirit than lethal spear
      thrusts in the body."

Crouther, Frank. University of North Carolina Daily Tar
   Heel, April 10, 1959, p. 2.
   Crouther presents a study which attempts to refute Sieg-
      fried Mandel's adverse review.

Dolin, Arnold. "Pyrotechnics," Saturday Review, XLII
   (February 21, 1959), 49.
   "I miss only the sense of being in the presence of real

people. "

Holley, F. S. "Nightmare Imprints on Each Page," Norfolk,
   Virginia Pilot, March 15, 1959, Sec. 5, p. 6.
   "The world of Nemerov as revealed here is peopled with
   phantoms--phantoms out of the abyss, to be sure--but
   still without substance."

Kirkus, XXVI (December 15, 1958), 926.
   "Nemerov's style has been wry, finely edged and intellec-
   tualized to the point of bloodlessness."

Mandel, Siegfried. "From a Nagging Impulse, A Chill,"
   New York Times, March 1, 1959, "Book Review" Sec.,
   p. 4.
   "If we were to read these stories backward, the final act
   would seem impossible; but Nemerov first creates a
   lifelike setting and from then on even the grotesque
   becomes real."

Mann, Charles. Library Journal, LXXXIV (February 1,
   1959), 535.
   Mann finds " . . . torment is tempered by Mr. Nemerov's
   range . . . "

Mayhew, Alice Ellen. "Quality of Life," Commonweal,
   LXIX (March 27, 1959), 673.
   "Mr. Nemerov's characters are, for the purpose of dra-
   matization, subjected to a sort of existential shock
   treatment to see whether they will, like living organ-
   isms, react to stimuli."

McClung, Denny. "Stories By Nemerov Probe Human Character," Roanoke, Virginia Times, March 1, 1959, Sec.
   B, p. 10.
   "Mr. Nemerov probes our innermost longings, our most
   sordid desires and fears, until it becomes absolutely
   uncomfortable."

Meras, Phyllis. "A Touch of the Macabre," New York
   Herald Tribune, March 1, 1959, "Book Review" Sec.,
   p. 8.
   "He describes those inexplicable, ever present impulses
   of all men, that shock almost all men, and shocking
   them, remain unexpressed."

Morrison, Don. "Nemerov Serves a Rich and Satisfying

Meal," Minneapolis Tribune, March 29, 1959, Sec. E, p.
6.
"Violence and death weave in and out of the book, but are
given a significance beyond that of mere shock value."

Nashville, Tennessean, June 21, 1959, Sec. C, p. 4.
"One may dislike the art-for-art's-sake function of his
work, but there is no denying the beauty of its form."

Olsen, Bruce. Louisville, Kentucky Courier Journal, March
22, 1959, Sec. 4, p. 7.
"The author is a moral abstractionist, essentially disinterested in character, society or ideas."

Tucker, Martin. Venture, III (Summer, 1959), 67.
" . . . the individual has been so truncated and flattened
that he has no hopes left. The only thing burning in
him is a guilt complex."

Virginia Quarterly Review, XXXV (Summer, 1959), lxxiv.
" . . . the paradoxical quality of human self-deception is
the main source of Mr. Nemerov's irony."

Wolf, Joseph. Best Sellers, XVIII (March 15, 1959), 482.
"Implausible, yes; yet Mr. Nemerov compensates with
irony and satire."

New and Selected Poems

Bewley, Marius. Partisan Review, XXVIII (January, 1961),
141.
Bewley finds some poems can be experienced "without the
effort of intellectual analysis, almost beyond thought's
dimension."

Bogan, Louise. New Yorker, XXVII (April 1, 1961), 129.
"The terror and Patmos of existence are not passed over;
there is a healthy turbulence at work under his un-
ruffled style."

Carruth, Hayden. "The Errors of Excellence," Nation,
CXCII (January, 1961), 63.
Nemerov's "poems present themselves, to me at least, in
the manner of praiseworthy newspaper editorials . . ."

Davidson, Peter. "Self-Revelation in the New Poetry,"

Atlantic Monthly, CCVIII (November, 1961), 171.
"The man revealed in these poems is an onlooker, a
    watcher whose perceptions are unruffled by the fury of
    involvement. "

Dickey, James. "The Death and the Keys of the Sensor,"
    Sewanee Review, LXIX (Spring, 1961), 331-332.
    " . . the enveloping emotion that arises from his writing
    is helplessness: the helplessness we all feel in the
    face of the events of our time, and of life itself: the
    helplessness one feels as one's legitimate but chroni-
    cally unfair portion in all the things that can't be as-
    suaged or explained. "

Gordon, Ambrose. Carleton Miscellany, II (Winter, 1961),
    116-120.
    "Out of the now and then one may construct a world--
    many worlds. The resulting patterns in Mr. Neme-
    rov's poems range from simple elegy to much more
    complicated arrangements, corresponding, as he tells
    us, to two different ways of looking at the world. "

Gunn, Thom. "Outside Fiction," Yale Review, L (Summer,
    1961), 586.
    "There is in fact a concentration of experience without the
    loss of richness and variety that concentration can in-
    volve. "

Hadas, Moses. "The Words of the Poet . . . Illuminate
    this Dream," New York Herald Tribune, July 30, 1961,
    "Book Review" Sec. , p. 7.
    "The poet rubs our nose in the stink and rawness and ex-
    citement of the twentieth century. "

Harman, Geoffrey. "Words and Things," Partisan Review,
    XXXII (Winter, 1965), 137-139.
    "In seeking to encompass the totality of being without
    metaphysics and by sheer tour de force of imagination,
    his thought runs to death, and beyond death to 'the
    other side.' "

Hughes, Rose Mae. "A Poet's View of Today's Man,"
    Columbia, Missouri Missourian, December 20, 1964,
    "Show Time" Sec. , p. 13.
    "Nature, he (Nemerov) feels, is where truth and atone-
    ment exist. "

Jacobson, Josephine. "Poets in Action," Prairie Schooner,
    XXXVI (Fall, 1962), 287.
    The collection's "core is its author's persistent preoccu-
      pation with the viable design--or its lack."

Kunitz, Stanley. "Some Poets of the Year and Their Lan-
    guage of Transformation," Harpers, CCXXIII (August,
    1961), 90.
    "The urbanity of the tone is often a mask for the depth of
      the feelings."

Lauter, Paul. "Poetry Demanding and Detached," New
    Leader, XLIV (May 15, 1961), 23.
    "With all his facility, or perhaps because of it, Nemerov
      lacks the consistent distinctiveness, the electric in-
      tensity of the best poetry in the academic group."

Morse, Samuel French. "Seven Poets, Present Tense,"
    Virginia Quarterly Review, XL (Spring, 1961), 291.
    " . . . these rather quiet but self-possessed poems have
      a good deal of staying power."

Ray, David. Epoch, X (Winter, 1961), 58.
    The poems "demonstrate the move away from insularity."

Rexroth, Kenneth. "A Stranger on Madison Avenue," New
    York Times, January 8, 1961, Sec. 7, p. 52.
    "These are formula poems in style and subject, but the
      formulas are unexceptional."

Smith, Ray. Library Journal, LXXXV (November 15, 1960),
    4151.
    Smith finds Nemerov has a "dialogue with himself."

Thompson, John. "A Catalogue of Poets," Hudson Review,
    XIII (Winter, 1960), 621.
    Nemerov's poetry is a disturbing quantity, for it presents
      "the fruits of observation rather than participation."
      Thompson presents his own troubled feelings about
      Nemerov.

The Next Room of the Dream

Burns, R. K. Library Journal, LXXXVIII (April 1, 1963),
    1535.
    "It is apparent that Mr. Nemerov is quite fatigued with

the cerebral writer and academic poet."

Carruth, Hayden. "Interim Report," Poetry, CII (September, 1963), 389-390.
"A proper conceit, as we know, consists of a joke and a moral; they must resist each other fiercely yet remain locked together--a sort of terrified embrace; and when they fall apart the joke becomes merely a joke, and the moral becomes merely a platitude. Which is what happens to too many of Nemerov's poems.

Davis, Paxton. "Poetry--Again on the Upswing?" Roanoke, Virginia Times, February 17, 1963, Sec. C, p. 8.
Nemerov is "a poet of enormous craft and great elegance rather than a true original, and to my mind it is not until the third section of this new volume that we hear the poet's own special voice . . ."

Dickey, William. "Hopes for Explosions," Hudson Review, XVI (Summer, 1963), 308-310.
Dickey finds Nemerov's irony an important technique.

Flint, R. W. New York Review of Books, I, No. 1 (1963), 26.
Flint presents a substantial analysis of the plays, Cain and Endor, as well as a brief identification of Nemerov as poet.

Johnson, W. R. Carleton Miscellany, IV (Spring, 1963), 120-124.
"Nemerov really is the best poet writing today."

Klausler, Alfred P. Christian Century, LXXX (March 20, 1963), 369.
Klausler finds the poems informed by "an incisive irony which undercuts the pretensions of present-day life and institutions."

Kunitz, Stanley. "Many Exertions, Some Excellences," New York Times, July 21, 1963, Sec. 7, p. 4.
Kunitz finds "what saves his (Nemerov's) poems from bloodless abstraction is the real care he has for 'daily things.'"

Ramsey, Paul. "A Dream Interpreted," Shenandoah, XV (Autumn, 1963), 65-67.
". . . the gentle and very modern malaise of self-effacing

irony . . . does infect in too high an intensity too
many of these poems."

Rosenthal, M. L. "Something That Might Simply Be," Reporter, XXIX (September 12, 1963), 54.
"The fine things that 'might simply be' do tend a bit to
get lost in the flood of other things."

Rubin, Louis. "Revelations of What is Present," Nation,
CXCVII (July 13, 1963), 38.
Nemerov's poems "provides that rare experience, in I. A.
Richards' words, of 'instants when the film of familiar-
ity and selfish solitude, which commonly hides nine-
tenths of life from the ordinary man, seems to be lifted
and he feels strangely alive and aware of the actuality
of existence.' "

Smith, W. J. "Modest, Original," Harpers, CCXXVI (September, 1963), 114.
" . . . a sane, intelligent and mature view enable him to
write on an unlikely subject."

Virginia Quarterly Review, XXXIX (Summer, 1963), xciv.
"The two plays, 'Endor' and 'Caine,' are stately in their
verbal movement and concise in their philosophical
statement.   Their future lies, however, not with the
theatre audience, but with the reader."

Endor

Jerome, Jud. "For Summer, A Wave of New Verse,"
Saturday Review, XLVI (July 6, 1963), 31-32.
"A poet who can do this can go on to greater things."

Knock, Stanley F. "Renewal of Illusion," Christian Century,
LXXX (January 16, 1963), 84.
Knock finds the focus is "man's sinful quest for knowledge
and the logical conclusion thereof."

Poetry and Fiction: Essays

Adams, Robert Martin.   Hudson Review, XVII (Spring, 1964),
146-148.
" . . . he is a critic in service to an ideal of poetry; and
even when he is writing about prose, it is the poetry

of the work he makes us see."

Campbell, Colin. "The Intuitive Critic," Christian Science
    Monitor, January 29, 1964, 9.
    "Much given to censuring rather than celebrating, and de-
    ficient perhaps as a theorist, Howard Nemerov is none
    the less one of the ablest critics in America . . ."

Chisholm, Scott. "Words as Keys to the Invisible," Saint
    Louis Post Dispatch, January 12, 1964, Sec. C, p. 4.
    " . . . so much of his own language succeeds in going
    beyond the mirror and laying bare what is often invis-
    ible to most of us . . . "

Foster, C. O. "Nemerov--An Urbane and Nimble Mind,"
    Bennington, Vermont Banner, April 2, 1964, Sec. 3, p. 4.
    "Mr. Nemerov offers fresh, exciting insight into the de-
    tails and compositions of particular works, at the same
    time developing the reader's understanding of a philoso-
    phy of literature, its ultimate values and purposes, and
    of the fine distinctions between the nature of art and the
    nature of other realities."

Howard, Richard. "Some Poets in Their Prose," Poetry,
    CIII (March, 1965), 400-403.
    Howard finds the book important in its ability to come to
    grips with modern poetry in a pleasing manner.

Howe, Irving. "A Cultivated Mind Willing to Bend to Work
    at Hand," New York Times, March 29, 1964, "Book Re-
    view," Sec., p. 5.
    Nemerov is "primarily a working critic, that is, a critic
    who devotes himself to careful description and judg-
    ment of individual writers and texts, rather than in-
    vestigating the grounds for judgment or the cultural con-
    text in which it occurs."

Malin, Irving. Books Abroad, XXXIX (Winter, 1965), 190.
    "The collection is unified: Nemerov is consistently aware
    of certain themes, especially the tension between mys-
    tery and concreteness, the sublime and the earthy."

O'Connor, William. "Notes on Seven Critics," Southern Re-
    view, New Series I (Winter, 1965), 235.
    Howard Nemerov "seems to read authors, especially his
    contemporaries, in a search for the possible."

Price, Martin. "New Books in Review," Yale Review,
    LIII (Summer, 1964), 592.
    Price finds the essays "seemed acute and shaped one's
        judgments, but they were hardly memorable in them-
        selves, exhibiting neither a bold personality nor a bold
        position."

Rosen, Roslyn. "A Design of Inner Sanity," Chicago Times,
    February 9, 1964, Sec. 4, p. 2.
    The reviewer compares the sensitivities of Nemerov to
        those of Nabokov.

Rubin, Louis D. "Well Worth the Saying," Kenyon Review,
    XXVI (Spring, 1964), 411-414.
    Rubin finds the controlling idea behind the collection is
        Nemerov's notion that "studying one's contemporaries,
        one gets an idea of what is possible as well as many
        ideas of what is not."

Simmons, Charles. "When the Muse Takes a Field Trip,"
    Saturday Review, XLVI (December 28, 1963), 40.
    Simmons presents a general appreciation of Nemerov's
        criticism.

Thompson, F. S. "Temperate Damnation and Praise,"
    Roanoke, Virginia Times, January 19, 1964, Sec. C, p.
    10.
    Thompson presents an appreciation of Nemerov's critical
        method.

Wallace, John. "Essays by Three Critics," Chicago Review,
    XVII, No. 4, 157-160.
    "We read this collection not for what it may tell us about
        his subjects, but for the revealed criteria of his own
        practice as a poet."

Weisinger, Herbert. "An Inside View," New Leader, XLVI
    (February 17, 1964), 21.
    Weisinger finds that Nemerov is interested in literature,
        criticism, and his own poetry, in such a manner that
        is "intensely self-aware of itself . . . and which grows
        with a special elan when it finds its own solutions to
        its own problems . . . it is constantly seeing itself
        see itself, constantly sharpening its sight. The result
        is an attitude of mind sophisticated and wry, concerned,
        not with storming the ramparts of earth and heaven,
        but with finding elegant solutions to problems so diffi-

cult technically that only those who know how difficult they
really are know how really elegant are the solutions. "

Journal of the Fictive Life

"Alias Felix Legers," [London] Times Literary Supplement,
April 28, 1966, 364.
The reviewer finds "these communings . . . opening a
third dimension of dream, memory and the acrostic
preoccupations of the literary imagination, prove their
own validity. "

Bergon, Frank. "A Writer Probes . . .," Boston Herald,
October 31, 1965, Sec. 6, p. 2.
"The value of such a journal lies in its revelation of the
artistic process as viewed by the artist. "

Burns, Richard K. Library Journal, XC (November 15,
1965), 4982.
The reviewer finds the book morbid, but powerful.

Choice, III (June, 1966), 310.
The journal is " . . . a not very original addendum to
the Kinsey report. "

Goldsmith, Richard. "A Poet Probes Self and Craft,"
Raleigh, North Carolina Observer, December 26, 1965,
Sec. 3, p. 3.
The reviewer concentrates on the organization of the
book.

Hicks, Granville. "Poetry From a Magic Reality," Saturday
Review, XLIX (June 11, 1966), 39.
The book is "a broad investigation of the creative process. "

Karlen, Arno. "Everything, And Yet . . .," New York
Times, January 16, 1966, Sec. 7, p. 6.
"It sits awkwardly between essay, confession, and docu-
ment. "

Kirkus, XXXIII (July 15, 1965), 741.
The book is a "diary-like aesthetic self-analysis" which
is unsatisfactory because of its superficiality.

MacKenzie, N. K. New York Times, November 19, 1965,
p. 37.

MacKenzie finds the book "may be the first non-book put
out by a respected novelist, poet and critic . . . it is
dull dreams described, and then analyzed . . . "

Matthews, W. P. Lillabulero, (Winter, 1967), 140-142.
"Falling somewhere between the diary and the notebook,
the journal records a mind engaged with itself."

Rubin, Louis D.   "What It's Like to be Father . . . Son
. . . and Husband," Washington, D. C. Star, October 24,
1965, Sec. D, p. 2.
Rubin traces Nemerov's search for identity in the book.

Schulze, E. J.   Michigan Quarterly Review, VI (Spring,
1967), 144-146.
"The Journal seems to be an elaborate and serious
'double entendre' built on the metaphor that 'Life is a
Story.' The credibility of the metaphor itself frees
him to steal from either of its sides to explain the
other."

Stepanchev, Stephen.   "The Order of Life," New Leader,
XVIII (November 22, 1965), 25.
In the journal, " . . . Nemerov sees his life as a poem
or a dream: the distinction blurs."

Van Duyen, Mona.   "The Poet as Novelist," Poetry, CIX
(February, 1967), 333.
"The book is a sort of 'live' drama of his wrestling with
his own Unconscious, which, after about two hundred
pages, he perceives to have blessed him with a kind
of 'novel.' It is also a sort of whodunnit of aesthetics,
involving its reader in a suspenseful attempt to answer
the question (asked in full awareness of the linkings
between life and art), 'Mommy, where do images come
from?' "

Virginia Quarterly Review, XLII (Winter, 1966), xxii.
"The poet and novelist Howard Nemerov has, in this
small penetrating, astonishing volume, set himself to
analyze by means of Freudian interpretation what, during a period when he found himself unable to write fiction, did in fact come into his dreams and waking mind,
and to see if the results of the examination would lead
him out of his stasis."

Poets on Poetry

Dembo, L. S. Criticism, VIII (Summer, 1966), 302.
　　Dembo finds the essays "satisfying a desire to hear the
　　poet speak of his own work . . . especially if he can
　　adjoin to the work some anecdotal richness or give
　　some hints of insight into the creative process."

Hecht, Anthony. "Poetry Chronicle," Hudson Review, XIX
　　(Summer, 1966), 330.
　　Of the poets represented, Hecht finds Nemerov the only
　　interesting essayist.

Kirkus, XXXIII (September 15, 1965), 1019.
　　" . . . none of the nineteen well-known contributors docu-
　　ment anything of importance."

Lentricchia, Frank. "Attitudes Toward Literature," Poetry,
　　CXI (May, 1967), 119.
　　"Poets on Poetry is most useful as a gloss to the work
　　of significant contemporary poets and as a testament
　　to the enduring power of a problem raised by Eliot:
　　the relationship of craft and medium to personal ex-
　　pression."

Untermeyer, Louis. "Each Man To His Own Metaphor,"
　　Saturday Review, XLIX (February 19, 1966), 45.
　　"The essays circle uncertainly around the question of
　　form, of content, of criticism, and that infinitely argu-
　　able topic: the meaning of poetry."

The Blue Swallows

Burke, Kenneth. American Scholar, (Summer, 1968), 518-
　　520.
　　"Repeatedly, I get the feeling of stopping, to be medita-
　　tively one with this or that nature in particular while
　　all the while there is a sense of all things moving on."

Carruth, Hayden. "In Their Former Modes," New York
　　Times, April 28, 1968, "Book Review" Sec., p. 7.
　　"The ironic method is 'double-entendre'; but when it is
　　used too much, double-meaning slides over again into
　　single-meaning; the literal meaning decays until it falls
　　into meaninglessness, while the emphasis shifts entire-
　　ly to the unspoken ironic meaning; and thus the poem

is left at odds with itself."

Conarroe, Joel. "Visions and Revisions," Shenandoah,
    (Summer, 1968), 78.
    "Implicit in all his work has been the assumption that art
    is vision, not dogma, and that the poet, in rederiving
    the possibilities of meaning from matter, has as his
    principal goal the task of rendering the highest possible
    justice to the visible world."

Davison, Peter. "New Poetry: The Generation of the Twen-
    ties," Atlantic Monthly, CCXXI (February, 1968), 142.
    The poems "explore the bewilderment of a mature and
    civilized man surveying the world without animus."

Dunn, Millard. "Through Poetry We 'Find the World,' "
    Roanoke, Virginia Times, September 8, 1968, Sec. C,
    p. 8.
    Dunn finds that Nemerov is able to "generate experience
    for the reader."

Galler, David. "Excellence and Victimization," Carleton
    Miscellany, (Summer, 1968), 111-112.
    "Over the years, Nemerov has managed to merge his
    self-satire and satire of the world through the matura-
    tion of a special tone--disarmingly colloqual and casu-
    al--and sustained irony."

Hecht, Anthony. "Writers' Rights and Reader's Rights,"
    Hudson Review, (April, 1968), 213-215.
    Nemerov "presents us with a highly intelligent and flexible
    viewpoint which is busily inspecting what is constantly
    passing for 'Civilization.' "

Lieberman, Lawrence. "New Poetry in Review," Yale Re-
    view, (Autumn, 1968), 140-141.
    Nemerov "stretches his mind to its limits, acknowledges
    thought-boundaries (as few philosophers are willing to
    do), and gracefully eases into adjacent planes of ex-
    perience, moving from idea to image, images that em-
    brace and interpret ideas more acutely than thought
    processes ordinarily can."

Meinke, Peter. "Nemerov Proves Again He Knows What
    He's Doing," St. Petersburg, Florida Times, October 20,
    1968, Sec. G, p. 5.
    Meinke finds Nemerov an existentialist.

_____ . "Twenty Years of Accomplishment," Florida
Quarterly, (October, 1968), 81-90.
While comparing the early and late poetry, Meinke finds
the collection is "another elucidation (another series
of examples) of what might be called a philosophy of
minimal affirmation."

Shapiro, Karl. "Showdown at City of Poetry," Chicago
Times, December 3, 1967, "Book Week" Sec., p. 5.
"The Nemerov poem is clipped like a thorn hedge: one
would not care to land in the middle of it."

Symons, Julian. "Visions," New Statesman, LXXV (February 9, 1968), 178.
"Nemerov's poems fall into two main groups, a metaphysical, fanciful kind about the connections of dream
and reality, and a kind in which ultimate truths and
ironies are revealed by direct story telling."

Williams, Miller. "Transactions With the Muse," Saturday
Review, (March 9, 1968), 32.
The poems show "the same fascination with the universe
of Einstein that has informed much of the poets best
work. He has carried on the search for a kind of unified field theory, some metaphor to bring time and
space, being and non-being, into harmony, and to say
where and what man is in the reality and illusion of
all this and how the illusion is real."

Index

The index includes authors cited, with the exception of the editors of anthologies. The numbers refer to pages.

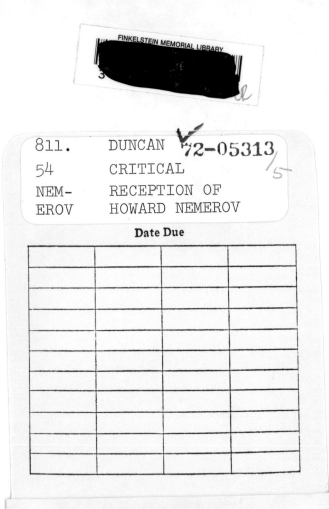